Strange Cults

ON THIS SITE IN FEDERAL HALL
APRIL 30 1789
GEORGE WASHINGTON
TOOK THE OATH AS THE FIRST PRES

Strange Cults

by Angus Hall

 Aldus Books London

Series Coordinator: John Mason
Design Director: Günter Radtke
Picture Editor: Peter Cook
Editor: Eleanor Van Zandt
Copy Editor: Maureen Cartwright
Research: Marian Pullen
General Consultant: Beppie Harrison

EDITORIAL CONSULTANTS:

**COLIN WILSON
DR. CHRISTOPHER EVANS**

**Frontispiece: followers of the Indian god Krishna.
Above: Colonel Simmons, founder of the Ku Klux Klan.**

Strange Cults

Man has always tended to join together with others, whether for worship, for philanthropy, or for the gratification of his desires. Whatever the ostensible motive, such groupings satisfy a basic need. By examining cults of many persuasions through the ages, this book helps to show the reasons for their lasting appeal.

Contents

1

The Lure of Cults

The year is 1897. Alfred Smythe, a man in his 50s, is a clerk in a London bank. Every weekday he sits at a massive mahogany desk, scrutinizing papers through a *pince-nez*, soberly manipulating the flow of pounds, shillings, and pence. At 6 o'clock sharp he puts on his overcoat and bowler hat, picks up his umbrella, and takes a cab to his house in Maida Vale, where he has a quiet supper with his wife, and then reads a bit before retiring.

On some evenings, however, our imaginary Mr. Smythe goes to an ordinary-looking house in central London known to himself and a few other people as the Isis-Urania

Right: blindfolded, a prospective member of the Order of the Golden Dawn kneels before the hierophant who conducts the initiation ceremony. As she is received into the Order, the blindfold is removed as a symbol of her emergence into the light. Most cults promise their members knowledge, enlightenment, and power denied to the uninitiated and it is this, combined with the sense of identity membership of such groups provides, that attracts so many to their ranks.

"What is the difference, if any, between a cult and a religion?"

Temple of the Golden Dawn. There, he enters a world totally different from the everyday world outside. Candles and incense create an atmosphere of mystery in the chamber, which is adorned with symbols: a rose, a cross, a truncated pyramid, a red dragon. Exotic words are spoken: *Neschamah, Ruach, Hierophant, Hegemon, Tristitia, Fortuna Minor*. In this world, the Mr. Smythe of the bank is transformed. He dons a long robe and colorful insignia, and he carries the Lotus Wand, a symbol of the magical Will. He and the other men and women in the room are Adepts. They work magic.

Mr. Smythe's colleagues at the bank would have hooted with laughter at the word "magic," for to the modern enlightened mind there is no such thing. Yet for the Adepts of the Golden Dawn, magic was not only real but of supreme importance. One initiate defined it as "the science and art of creating changes in consciousness." The members believed that by studying the teachings of the Order, culled from ancient mystical writings, and by performing its elaborate rituals they could escape the bondage of the material world and be "brought to the Light." They believed that mystical forces and supernatural intelligences are at work in the universe and that the trained Adept could invoke these forces and intelligences.

The Golden Dawn no longer exists as an organization— although its teachings continue to be studied. One of its most famous members was the Irish poet W. B. Yeats. In a pamphlet concerning the Order's system of examinations, Yeats expressed eloquently the purpose of the Order as he saw it: "the passing . . . from one degree to another is an evocation of the Supreme Life, a treading of a symbolic path, a passage through a symbolic gate, a climbing towards the light which it is the essence of our system to believe flows continually from the lowest of the invisible Degrees to the highest of the Degrees that are known to us. It matters nothing whether the Degrees above us are in the body or out of the body, for none the less must we believe the light flows downward continually. . . ."

In Yeats's words we can glimpse something of the appeal that cults have for so many people. Most cults promise the initiate a fuller life. By studying the cult's teachings and participating in its rituals, the person can transcend the mechanical, mundane life he normally leads and link up with some source of power.

Of course the same applies to what we call a religion. Here we encounter a sticky problem of definition: what is the difference, if any, between a cult and a religion? There is no simple answer. Drawing a distinction between a cult and a religion is relatively easy when we consider cults that regard themselves as supplementary to religion. The Templars, an order of knights in medieval Europe, were at least nominal Christians (although some have been excommunicated); and they were initially formed to further the goals of the Crusaders. Likewise, Freemasonry includes many practicing members of various faiths.

Distinguishing between a cult and a religion is also relatively easy in the case of cults that hold no belief in a supernatural power. No one would be likely to regard the Hell's Angels—to take an extreme example—as a religion. Yet the Angels are unmistakably a cult, with their own initiation ceremonies, marriage

Left: the Irish poet W.B. Yeats was throughout his life fascinated by mysticism and the occult. In his search for spiritual enlightenment he joined the Order of the Golden Dawn, and in a pamphlet described eloquently the symbolic meaning and purpose of the cult.

Below: Aleister Crowley, magician and occultist, leads a group of his disciples, in a photograph published in the Magazine *Equinox*. Twelve years earlier, in 1898, Crowley had been initiated into the Order of the Golden Dawn but he had not long remained a member. After leaving the Order, he pursued his search for spiritual and mystical knowledge through various sects that he founded himself.

Left: the Earl of Zetland as Worshipful Grand Master of the British Freemasons, a drawing made in 1869. From its humble origins in the craft guilds of medieval England, Freemasonry has grown into a worldwide movement of unimpeachable respectability, a cult that has become as much a part of the establishment as organized religion in many of the countries where it flourishes. Yet the aims and work of the movement remain shrouded in secrecy, hidden behind the closely guarded ritual, involving strange costumes and complicated ceremonies, which forms as vital a part of Freemasonry as rites of the Order of the Golden Dawn did of that cult.

customs, and an implicit—if repulsive—set of beliefs. On a more socially acceptable level, some cults seek to help the individual realize his own potential, but as they do not subscribe to any belief in a Supreme Being or supernatural beings, they are not considered religions.

The distinctions begin to blur when we look at some of the groups that do believe in God and call themselves religions but approach God in unorthodox ways. But who is to say what is unorthodox? To most Roman Catholics, all Protestant denominations are unorthodox; to the average Methodist or Episcopalian, the Jehovah's Witnesses are unorthodox; and

Above: British Hell's Angels, unwashed and unshaven, astride the motorcycle or "stallion" that is the symbol of their cult. Far removed from the seekers after enlightenment of the Order of the Golden Dawn, or from the semireligious Freemasons, the Hell's Angels are nevertheless unmistakably a cult, with their own initiation and marriage ceremonies, and their own highly individual beliefs.

Left: obscure religious cults now proliferate in the United States. This lay preacher of the snake-handler sect holds a poisonous rattlesnake to prove his faith in God's ability to protect him from harm. At a later meeting, however, he was bitten by the venomous snake and died.

nearly all branches of Christendom would look askance at the snake-handlers or Holiness groups of the southern United States. And yet the snake-handler obviously believes as sincerely in his faith as the Catholic believes in his, and probably believes he has found the true way, missed by the so-called "orthodox" religions. He would not call himself a cultist.

To most citizens of ancient Rome, the followers of Jesus of Nazareth were a cult—one of many. The Romans were tolerant of cults. Besides the native gods, they welcomed any number of foreign deities, and devotees of these gods enjoyed freedom of worship. But all people, whatever their religion, were obliged to worship the emperor as well, and this the Christians refused to do. They did not regard themselves as just another cult, and they refused to be treated as such—with consequences everyone knows.

Leaving aside the question of the truth of Christianity, we can see that the early Christians shared many attributes of other cults, including modern ones. They had discovered a new truth—one of which most people were ignorant. This made them feel "special." The feeling of being set apart from the rest of the world was reinforced by the intermittent persecutions they suffered. They looked to each other—as well as to God—for their support. This inward-looking solidarity is a marked charac-

11

Left: Christians at worship in the catacombs of Rome. The early Christians were regarded by both Jews and Romans as members of a cult religion. The persecution of the Romans forced them to hold their services in secret, and this need for secrecy meant that early Christianity did indeed bear many of the features that are today associated with cults. Right: a procession to welcome spring goes through the streets of pre-Christian Rome. The children taking part carry bunches of flowers to symbolize the year's rebirth. The Roman Empire was generally tolerant of cults, provided that cult members—unlike the Christians—also accepted the Roman Empire's own religion.

teristic of most groups that we would call cults (although it is also characteristic of almost any minority group). The secrecy the early Christians were forced to observe heightened their sense of being a distinct group. Secrecy, concerning the membership or the beliefs and rituals, has been an important factor in the life of many cults.

As soon as Christianity became the official religion of the Roman Empire, it shed these cultlike attributes. For centuries thereafter, it was simply the faith of civilized Europe, practiced by everyone except the Jews, who were ostracized, and isolated groups of heretics, such as the Albigensians of southern France, who were ruthlessly suppressed.

Numerous splinter groups in medieval Europe challenged the teachings of the Church, but few made much headway. A climate conducive to cults—such as we have in the West today—did not exist. Apart from the sheer power of the Church, which made starting a cult a risky enterprise, there was the fact that the Church itself satisfied those needs that inspire a person to join a cult. It offered him a way to approach the supernatural, a moral discipline for his life, and an elaborate ritual full of symbolic meanings. Moreover, the original teachings of Christianity were gradually embellished with a host of legends concerning the saints—their miracles, their martyrdoms, their relics. Devotion to particular saints—chiefly, of course, the Virgin Mary—satisfied people's need for more of what we might crudely call "human interest" in their religion. In effect, cults grew up within the Church instead of outside it. In another dimension, the various monastic orders offered some Christians a special way of worshiping God, as well as a special identity and sense of belonging within the larger community of the Church.

Today, all this remains true for devout Catholics; their Church fills needs that other people seek in cults. It is also true in different ways for devout Protestants and for members of the other major world religions. In the case of mainstream Protestantism, much of the ritual has been pared away and the cults of

the saints eliminated. Even without these emotionally and esthetically satisfying features, Protestant Christianity remains for many people a completely fulfilling belief and a way of life. (Nevertheless, the large number of Protestants who are Freemasons may indicate a need for ritual that is not satisfied within their Church—even allowing for the fact that much of the Masons' appeal is social.)

Outside the strongly Catholic countries, the picture in the West is predominantly a contrast between those who profess no religion and those who belong to new religious sects and cults. The situation in England will serve as an example. The Established Anglican Church is the largest in terms of nominal membership, but only a few of these members attend its services. For most English people the Church is simply a part of the cultural landscape, and they rarely notice it. This is partly due to the fact that the Anglican Church is so eminently respectable, so identified with the middle and upper classes (not that many of these people are active communicants) that working-class people feel it has nothing to say to them. And although its stately

Below: many of the traditions of pre-Christian cults were taken up by the Christian religion, which incorporated them into its own ritual. This Polish procession on the feast day of Corpus Christi is a modern version of age-old midsummer festivities and the children, like the Roman ones of long ago, use flowers in their celebration.

ritual continues to satisfy many people—both spiritually and esthetically—it strikes others as cold and lacking in mystery.

By contrast, the Order of Bards, Ovates, and Druids, whose colorful gatherings provide plenty of material for British newspapers, seems to offer plenty of mystery. The Druids—as they are called, for short—are the spiritual descendants of the priests of the ancient Celtic religion. Like all ancient religions Druidism was pantheistic, and it particularly reverenced the sun and moon. Aspiring priests, who were trained in pre-Roman Britain, spent years memorizing long poems containing Druidical teachings.

The Druids seem to have had some knowledge of astronomy, and ceremonies marking the summer and winter solstices and the spring and autumn equinoxes are a prominent part of the observances of modern Druids. On these occasions they gather at certain sacred places including Stonehenge, Glastonbury Tor, and Parliament Hill overlooking London. Wearing blue, green, or white robes, according to their status, they form circles, and to the sound of a trumpet announce the new season. At the winter solstice, held indoors, Celtic music played on the harp and a sword dance symbolizing death and resurrection form part of the ceremony. Modern Druids also practice meditation to train their higher faculties—an emphasis found in many of the popular cults of our time.

The Druid revival, like the revival of witchcraft, is a symptom of the dissatisfaction people feel with a life devoid of mystery. Although some people believe in a natural world governed entirely by impersonal forces, many others find such a philosophy rather comfortless. In particular, they are disturbed by the idea that with death they will cease to exist. Moreover, their lives on earth often seem mechanical and monotonous. Impersonal forces—now often literally impersonal, with the computer revolution—seem to be in charge of their lives. Bored in school, they go on to be bored in their jobs, and after the first glow of love and marriage has worn off they settle down to being bored with each other. Worries about money, worries about health, worries about children, and worries about old age haunt their days. The happy moments and the occasional feelings of achievement cannot quite banish the suspicion that it is all, truly, a treadmill to oblivion.

Now suppose a person who feels this way is told that there are *personal* forces at work in nature and that he can partake of their power. He can be initiated into the mysteries of nature, as his ancestors were in ancient times. He can transcend the limitations of his own body, look into the future, cure illnesses, influence other people, and not only survive death but perhaps also live again on earth. Such promises are among those offered by the numerous cults of the present day. Their potential appeal for a person who has lost his sense of identity is obvious. It is no use telling such a person that just down the street at St. Cuthbert's he can gain a sense of identity and communicate with the Creator of the universe. At St. Cuthbert's he will find a handful of elderly ladies and gentlemen listlessly singing the gloomier 19th-century hymns to a God who seems not so much the Creator of the universe as a benign but strict headmaster.

How much more exhilarating to don a blue robe and welcome

Above: William McAuliffe as Archdruid, a drawing made in 1911. The Druids were the priests of the ancient Celtic religion of pre-Roman Britain but Druidism, which involved human sacrifice, was outlawed by the Romans in the 1st century A.D. The religion survived in the remoter parts of western Britain, however, and following the rediscovery of classical texts in which it was described, it enjoyed a revival as a cult religion. By 1911 William McAuliffe was the leader of 300,000 British Druids. Right: modern Druids celebrate the summer solstice in Stonehenge. In 1964, British Druidism was reformed as the Order of Bards, Ovates, and Druids, under whose auspices Druidism has become one of the most prominent sects in the British Isles. It is probably the mystical and ritual aspects of the cult that constitute its appeal to present-day members.

Above: the Rosicrucian Order has undergone several transformations since it was first founded early in the 17th century, and the first Rosicrucian mystics would probably have had little in common with members of the Order today. This symbolic drawing dates from 1618, in the early years of the movement, and could have been interpreted only by an initiate of the cult. It represents the Temple of the Rosy Cross, standing on wheels to signify that it can go anywhere in the world, and suspended by a rope from heaven to show that it is moved by the will of God.

Right: *The Virgin of the Lilies*, painted by Carlos Schwabe, was exhibited in Paris in 1897 at the last of six "Salons de la Rose Croix" where symbolic paintings were shown. The salons were the inspiration of Josephin Péladan, who founded his own Rose-Croix Order of Catholicism—an Order that, however, had nothing in common with 17th-century mystical Rosicrucianism but its name.

the summer at sunrise on Glastonbury Tor! Even more exhilarating to shed one's clothes and dance naked around the fire at night in the witches' coven to invoke the Great Mother.

Cults that try to revive the ancient, pagan beliefs form only a small part of the cult scene. Many of today's cultists care little, if anything, for ritual or for the past. One of the most widespread of modern cults, the Ancient Mystical Order Rosae Crucis (founded in 1915), bears little resemblance to the original Rosicrucian Order founded in Germany in the 17th century, or to later embodiments of its mystical teachings, such as the Golden Dawn. The modern Rosicrucians, who number some 60,000 in the United States alone, follow courses of study intended to help the common man function more effectively in the workaday world. In one of the organization's leaflets, a salesman is quoted as saying that by applying Rosicrucian principles he has been able to "knock the 't' out of 'can't.'" Members are not obliged to attend lodge meetings, and may progress through the degrees of the Order by private study, which need not take more than an hour or two each week. The lessons include such potentially challenging subjects as "the mysteries of time and space; the human consciousness; and the nature of matter," dealt with in terms comprehensible to the average person.

The headquarters and Supreme Temple of the modern Rosicrucian Order are located in San José, California—which comes as no surprise, for California is the magnet for cults of every kind. Southern California, in particular, has long attracted people who are searching for a new approach to life, as well as those who exploit the searchers for their private gain. One of these was Guy W. Ballard, who, in the 1930s, organized a cult called "I Am."

Claiming to be inspired by a spirit called the "Ascended

Below: the Egyptian museum at the headquarters of modern Rosicrucianism in San José, California. Through studies that combine science with occultism, present-day Rosicrucians aim to realize their full potential as human beings, progressing upward through the Order as they do so, somewhat in the same way as Freemasons do.

Above: stage setting used at "I Am" cult meeting in the United States. Despite such quasi-religious trappings, the organization seems to have been little more than a means of enriching its founder, Guy Ballard, and it was eventually charged with fraud. Above right: Guy Ballard's wife and son leave the Los Angeles courtroom where three of the "I Am" leaders had been acquitted of fraud. Ballard had died before the case came to trial.

Master Saint Germain," who had given him "electric essence" and "concentrated energy" as food and drink, Ballard promised to pass on to his followers powers that would bring them the treasures of the earth. But the treasure flowed in one direction— into Ballard's pockets, from the sales of books, phonograph records, icons, and other paraphernalia of the cult. Eventually the organization was charged with using the mails to defraud. With this scandal and the death of Ballard in 1939, "I am" collapsed.

Still in existence is the Four Square Gospel movement, founded in Los Angeles in the 1920s by a young Canadian named Aimée Semple McPherson. Endowed with a charismatic personality, Aimée quickly gathered a large following. At her

Angelus Temple, built at a cost of $1,500,000, she packed them in with a mixture of old-time evangelism, faith healing, and showbiz. Services would begin with Aimée, clad in white gown and long robe, walking down a circular ramp with a spotlight trained on her, to the music of recorded choirs. On one occasion she varied the procedure by roaring down the ramp on a motorcycle, screeching to a halt, and shouting, "Stop! You're headed straight for hell!" In her way, Aimée was applying the maxim of stripper Gypsy Rose Lee: "You've gotta have a gimmick." After Aimée died in 1944, the Four Square Gospel lost much of its impetus, although it still numbers 113,000 followers in the United States and abroad.

Many cults have come and gone since the heyday of Aimée Semple McPherson. Some are based loosely on the major world religions, particularly Eastern religions. There is a widespread conviction in the West today that the East, especially India, holds the key to true wisdom, which our active, competitive society has ignored. And so from Los Angeles to

Right: Aimée Semple McPherson, leader of the Four Square Gospel movement, in battle with the "Gorilla of Ungodliness." Short films were often used at the Four Square Gospel movement's services to drive home the cult's message. The more sensational scenes— like this one—combined with Aimée's strong personality and unorthodox approach, gave the movement so much publicity that it built up a huge following both in the United States and abroad.

Drawing by Opie; © 1973 The New Yorker Magazine, Inc.

Above: Dr. Timothy Leary,
founder of the League for Spiritual
Discovery. The league's initials,
LSD, also stand for the drug
lysergic acid, which Leary and his
followers use to promote their
spiritual explorations. From such
movements as Leary's grew the
hippie drug culture of the 1960s.

Munich we find young people shaving their heads and donning saffron-yellow robes to chant "Hare Krishna" on crowded streets, while in any number of quiet rooms, businessmen and housewives learn yoga and practice Eastern techniques of meditation.

Some of the popular cults of today are quite devoid of mystical or supernatural content. They concentrate on the attainment of physical or mental health. A typically American contribution to cultism is sensitivity training. This is an intensified form of group therapy that promises to help a person lose his inhibitions and relate to others in a direct, no-holds-barred way. At the Esalen Institute, located in Big Sur, California, encounter groups of men and women sometimes sit nude in a shallow swimming pool, becoming aware of their own bodies and learning to communicate with each other free of the artificial barriers symbolized by clothing. Although these are temporary gatherings, intended to help the person function in the world at large, encounter groups nevertheless resemble cults in the fervent belief of the initiates that they have found a new way of living. Occasionally, converts to belief in sensitivity training adopt it as a full-time way of life. A California advertising executive was so transformed by his experience at the Esalen Institute that he abandoned his $100,000-a-year job to work at the Institute as a dishwasher.

Encounter groups are, of course, simply the latest manifestation of the psychology cult that has been with us for most of this century. Without meaning to denigrate the contributions of psychologists and psychoanalysts in helping disturbed people cope with life, one can see that for many people psychoanalysis has become the True Faith—the way and the truth. In some affluent circles in the United States, people have their children analyzed almost as a matter of course, irrespective of whether the child has shown any signs of potential neurosis.

At this point, we have stretched our concept of a cult to include what is more a set of attitudes (although a visit to the psychiatrist does have its ritualistic aspects, and the "collection" figures prominently). Much more in the cult mainstream are the "feedback churches."

Found mainly in Southern California, under such names as The Holy Feedback Church and the Church of the Sacred Alpha,

these organizations are dedicated to helping people attain a special state of mind called the alpha rhythm. The activity of the brain can be monitored by means of a device that registers the activity in the form of a wavy line called an electroencephalogram, or EEG. When the brain is in a relaxed yet attentive state, a distinctive pattern called alpha waves appears on the EEG. Psychologists have discovered that people can to some extent control some bodily functions, such as heartbeat or body temperature, if they can observe at each moment what is happening. Thus, if a person is linked up with an EEG and can see when his brain produces alpha waves, he can in time learn to produce alpha waves at will. The EEG feeds back the information that the person is himself feeding into the machine. The point of the discipline is to expand one's capacity for meditation.

Although meditation is inherently a private activity, the cultists have brought it into a group context. At the feedback churches, disciples can link up with each other and provide mutual support in the quest for enlightenment.

The feedback church thus combines two dominant themes in modern cultism: relating to others and exploring the potential of the mind. Confidence in the power of rational, logical thinking as the way to truth—a cherished Western belief since the 18th century—is increasingly being challenged by advocates of the mystical approach to truth. A cult that offers people a new way to apprehend the mysteries of the universe is sure of a following.

In the early 1960s the Western world rocked with the discovery of a new, quick, and drastic way to expand the mind: LSD. The white-coated laboratory workers who first distributed the little capsules of lysergic acid to volunteers and methodically noted the subjects' physiological and psychological responses could hardly have imagined that within a year or two these little capsules would be the center of a new religion. In a Victorian mansion in the Hudson Valley, an ex-Harvard professor, Dr. Timothy Leary, formed the League for Spiritual Discovery. Leary and his disciples regarded LSD as a "sacrament," capable of bringing about a mystical union of the self and the universe.

At the same time, out on the West Coast, a young novelist named Ken Kesey also discovered the pleasures of the drug and soon became the leader of a group of hippies who called themselves the Merry Pranksters and who were dedicated to the

Above: a "Jesus March" in Rochester, New York. With the emergence of the latest mass religious cult, the wheel has turned full circle, for, in accordance with their name, the Jesus People preach a return to the teachings of Jesus Christ. Their beliefs, although based on the Bible, are seldom wholly compatible with orthodox Christianity.

gospel of LSD. In his book *The Electric Kool-Aid Acid Test,* journalist Tom Wolfe tells the bizarre saga of the Pranksters—their psychedelic paradise in La Honda, California, their rambunctious travels in a multicolor painted bus, and their fervent belief in the liberating power of the "new experience." The appalled citizens of Middle America who watched the Pranksters roar through town in their outlandish bus, whooping and gesticulating, would have been stunned to learn that these apparent mental cases considered themselves missionaries. Through LSD they had attained a sense of being, in Wolfe's words, "a vessel of the divine, of the All-one." The acid-heads shared with the great mystics of history the conviction that they had discovered a transcendental truth. "What they all saw in . . . a flash," wrote Wolfe, "was the solution to the basic predicament of being *human*, the personal *I, Me,* trapped, mortal and helpless, in a vast impersonal *It,* the world around me. Suddenly!—All-in-one! flowing together, *I* into *It,* and *It* into *Me,* and in that flow I perceive a power, so near and so clear, that the whole world is blind to . . . The—*so-called*! friends—rational world. If only *they*, Mom&Dad&Buddy&Sis, dear-but-square ones, could but know the . . . supreme moment. . . ."

In their zeal to bring others into the experience, the Pranksters once served cups of Kool-Aid laced with LSD to a gathering of some 200 people at the Youth Opportunities center near Watts. "It was a prank, partly, but mainly it was the natural culmination of the Acid Tests. It was a gesture, it was sheer generosity giving all this acid away, it was truly turning on the world. . . ."

Some of the joy began to go out of the LSD cult in the late 1960s. Bad trips, suicides, disquieting news of birth defects as a result of pregnant women taking the drug were some of the factors that contributed to its decline. As LSD lost its hold on the hippie population, some of the former acid freaks discovered a new "high": Jesus.

The Jesus Freaks are supposed to have first appeared on Sunset Strip in Los Angeles in 1967. Since then, the movement has swept the United States and other Western countries, attracting young followers from all segments of society, to the astonishment and occasional dismay of the orthodox. The movement now includes several subgroups, from the flamboyant hippies who identify with Jesus as an "outlaw" and promote the Gospel via earsplitting rock music, to the neatly dressed young students whose evangelism is an outgrowth of conservative Protestantism. There is even a Catholic wing, the "Catholic Pentecostals," who combine a rigidly orthodox form of Catholic doctrine with the spontaneous enthusiasm of Pentecostal religion and a strong distrust of the hierarchy of their own Church. Many of the Jesus People live in communes, in which they try to practice Christianity in simple surroundings.

Those who like irony will relish the spectacle of the former acid-heads sparking off a Christian revival, preaching the Gospel to a nominally Christian "straight" society that regarded these same rebels as bearers of a virulent disease. Ironic it certainly is. A sign of hope for the declining Christian religion—perhaps. A passing fad—perhaps. In the history of cults it is far from the strangest manifestation of the endless quest for a new way of life.

Above: at this mass baptism of Jesus People, several hundred men and women were baptized by total immersion in the waters of the Pacific Ocean. Such scenes of conversion recall the Bible's account of early Christian baptisms. Today's Jesus People want to bypass the established Christian Church and 20th-century materialism and to follow the teachings of Jesus Christ.

Left: a Californian teenager gives the "Jesus sign" during a mass baptism. This gesture, with its upward-pointing index finger signifying that the only way to salvation lies in Jesus, is now recognized as a universal symbol of the Jesus cult. It is still too early to say whether the vigor and enthusiasm of these new followers of Jesus will challenge and change established Christianity as did that earlier "return to Christ," the Reformation of over 550 years ago.

Cults
of Violence

On the afternoon of August 9, 1969, the front pages of American newspapers announced that in a secluded ranch-style house near Los Angeles five people, including the movie actress Sharon Tate, had been slaughtered. Summoned by an hysterical housekeeper, the police had found, first, the body of a young man named Steven Parent, shot and stabbed several times, lying in his car in the driveway. On the lawn they next found the bodies of Abigail Folger and Jay Frykowski, friends of Sharon Tate. Their bodies bore multiple stab wounds, and Frykowski had been shot twice. Inside the house, in the living room, lay the slashed

Above: a Thug captured by the British, a painting made by an Indian court artist in about 1842. Cults glorifying violence, whether for religious, political, or material ends, have existed in various cultures at different times. The Thugs, a secret sect of ritual killers, flourished in India for hundreds of years. Right: Kali, Hindu goddess of death, clutches a bloodstained knife as she stands over a victim. The Thugs worshiped Kali, believing their murders honored her.

"A story so bizarre as to defy belief"

bodies of hairstylist Jay Sebring, who had also been shot in the ribs, and Sharon Tate. At the time of her death, Miss Tate, who was married to film director Roman Polanski, was expecting her first child.

A few months later, in the course of what became the longest trial in American history, there emerged a story so bizarre as to defy belief. The murders at the Polanski residence had been committed by three members of a group calling themselves the "Family," followers of a 34-year-old ex-convict named Charles Manson. On the night following the murder of Sharon Tate and her friends, two of the killers and another member of the Family—supervised this time by Manson himself—had also murdered supermarket chain owner Leno LaBianca and his wife Rosemary. Between them the LaBiancas had been stabbed 67 times. When the murderers had finished stabbing their victims they had gone to the kitchen and enjoyed a snack of watermelon and chocolate milk. They had also fed the LaBiancas' dogs: the Family believed in being kind to animals.

None of the seven victims in the Tate-LaBianca murders was known to the assailants. They had been killed because Manson had decided, "Now is the time for helter skelter."

And what was "helter skelter"? This was to be the last war on earth. In the words of Susan ("Sadie Mae") Atkins, one of the killers, "It would be all the wars that have ever been fought built one on top of the other. . . . You can't conceive of what it would be like to see every man judge himself and then take it out on every other man all over the face of the earth." It would be a racial war, between whites and blacks, Manson believed, from which the blacks would emerge triumphant. Then they would gradually learn that they were incapable of governing and would turn over the government to Manson.

Manson hated the blacks (there is a possibility that his father, whom Manson never knew, had Negro blood), but he also hated the white "establishment." He harbored a resentment against the Hollywood show business world because it had not recognized his abilities as a pop singer. Manson thought of himself as—among other things—the "fifth Beatle." In the lyrics of some of the Beatles' songs he found peculiarly significant phrases. One of the songs was entitled "Helter Skelter," and Manson claimed to hear in this song the Beatles asking him to call them in London. In another number, "Revolution 9," Manson heard the Beatles whispering "Charlie, Charlie, send us a telegram." The title of this song linked up nicely with Manson's favorite bit of Scripture, the Book of Revelation, Chapter IX, which contains the passage: "Neither repented they of their murders, nor of their sorceries, nor of their fornications, nor of their thefts." He would repeat these words over and over again to the Family, instilling in them the belief that killing was right. Death was inconsequential, Manson believed. It was only a "change," for the soul could not die.

He despised women. Their only purpose, he often said, was to serve men and bear children. But he found it useful to have them in the Family as bait to attract the men. Every female member of the Family had to be willing to copulate with anyone immediately, on Manson's command. He boasted of his own sexual

Above: Charles Manson, ex-convict, hippie leader, failed pop
musician—and mass murderer. An early life spent in and out of
penal institutions produced in Manson a hatred for the establishment,
for authority, and for wealth. Rejecting society, he led a group of
young men and women—his "Family"—out into the California desert.
There, despite their communal and somewhat squalid existence,
the Family learned to revere Manson as a god, to be followed
and obeyed unquestioningly, no matter what he might ask. Meanwhile,
Manson meditated on the form his revenge on society should take.

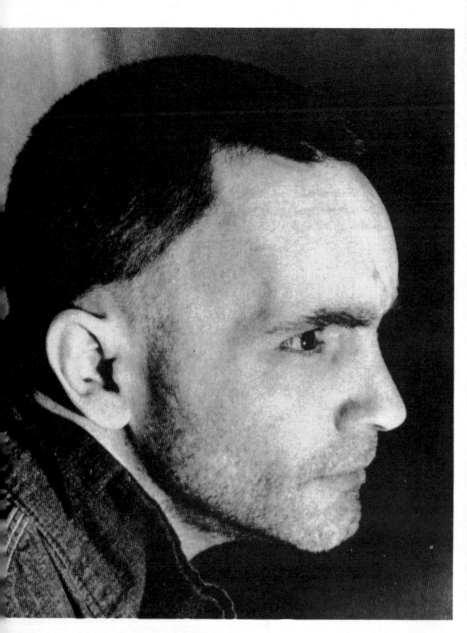

Above: Charles Manson after his conviction for the murders of actress Sharon Tate and friends at her home, and of store-owner Leno LaBianca and his wife. Manson attempted to revenge himself on society by eliminating those elements in it that he despised, and such was the awe in which he was held by the Family that he was willingly obeyed even when his order was to kill. Manson and the Family were as defiant after his conviction as before.

prowess, yet admitted that he preferred men. Most of the time he wanted the women out of sight, engaged in chores around the run-down ranch where the Family lived. Those who had children were forbidden to talk to them except in gibberish—so as to prevent their forming close attachments. Manson frequently beat up his women and threatened to cut off their breasts.

The women loved him. More accurately, they worshiped him. Describing one beating from Manson, Stephanie Schram said, "I never wanted him to hit me, but I wanted to be made to see in a different way. And the only way Charlie knew how to make me see in a different way was to do that." Susan Atkins told Prosecuting Attorney Vincent Bugliosi that Manson was "the only man I have ever met . . . that is a complete man. He will not take back-talk from a woman. He will not let a woman talk him into doing anything. He is a man."

More than a man, he was, they believed, Jesus Christ. Manson never actually said he was Christ, but he did say that he had

Left: Charles Manson depicted as the Devil, with his female followers groveling at his feet. Manson called himself the Devil, Satan, or Soul, yet he also said that he had lived 2000 years ago and died on the cross—obviously implying that he was Jesus Christ. He despised women, regarding them merely as servants and as a means of gratifying the sexual desires of men.

Below: female members of the Family squatted daily outside the courtroom where Manson was on trial, and when Manson shaved his head after being declared guilty, so did the girls outside. Manson might despise women, but to these girls he was not only their leader, but their god.

lived before, 2000 years ago, and had died on the cross. The implication was clear enough. Yet he also referred to himself as the Devil, or Satan, or Soul.

Confusion of identity was a striking feature of the Family's mentality. It was not just a matter of their various nicknames and aliases; it was a submersion of one's individuality, becoming one with the group mind. They were part of Manson and he was part of them. "I became Charlie," said Family member Paul Watkins. "Everything I once was, was Charlie. There was nothing left of me any more. And of all the people in the Family, there's nothing left of them any more, they're all Charlie too."

The confusion of identity was matched by a confusion of love and hate. In prison, Susan Atkins tried to explain to a fellow inmate how she had managed to kill Sharon Tate: "I loved her, and in order for me to kill her I was killing part of myself when I killed her. . . . You have to have a real love in your heart to do this for people."

Above: Aleister Crowley, occultist and magician, founded an English branch of O.T.O., Ordo Templi Orientis, a German occult organization devoted to sexual magic. By the 1960s, O.T.O. was active in California, where its leaders forged it into a hate force not unlike Manson's Family.

Above right: part of a mural painted by Crowley at his "Abbey of Thelema" in Cefalu, Sicily. Thelema, which means "Do what thou wilt," was a "religion" intended by Crowley to supercede Christianity. Part of its doctrine was that man had the right to kill those who thwarted his desires—a belief that helps to explain Crowley's appeal to the death cults of California.

Left: Bobby Beausoleil, rock musician and part of Manson's Family. At the time of the Tate and LaBianca murders, Beausoleil was already under arrest, charged with stabbing to death music teacher Gary Hinman. The words "Do what thou wilt," which appear on the door behind Beausoleil in this photograph, formed the credo not only of the Family but also of many of the other California hippie groups of the late 1960s.

Partial explanations for this lunatic mentality can be found by examining the individual histories of its members. Manson himself spent his childhood being passed around among various relatives and neighbors, learning to steal, being put into and escaping from corrective schools. At the age of 16 he was described by a caseworker as "aggressively antisocial." Other members of the Family had impaired relationships with their own families and emotional disturbances that Manson exploited. As Prosecuting Attorney Bugliosi pointed out in his book *The Manson Murders*: "Nearly all had within them a deep-seated hostility toward society and everything it stood for which pre-existed their meeting Manson." What Manson did was to bring to the surface "their latent hatred, their inherent penchant for sadistic violence, focusing it on a common enemy, the establishment. He depersonalized the victims by making them symbols. It is easier to stab a symbol than a person."

But Manson and his Family did not operate in a vacuum. The environment in which the Family was formed, the drug sub-culture, the whole grotesque assortment of violence freaks, Satan-worshipers, and blood-sacrifice cultists that flourishes in California helped to prepare the way for "helter skelter."

For example, there was the Kirké Order of Dog Blood, whose members worshiped a supposed reincarnation of the goddess Circe—or Kirké—and who sacrificed animals on secluded beaches near Los Angeles. Evidence suggests that some members of Manson's Family participated in these rituals, no doubt finding some way to reconcile these atrocities with their principle of kindness to animals.

More widespread was the Ordo Templi Orientis, or O.T.O.,

Above: Manson as folk hero. The murderer was supported not only by the members of the Family, but also by some sections of the underground culture—the underground magazine *Tuesday's Child* even nominated him "Man of the Year." Its views are shared by few: according to the San Francisco *Chronicle*, Manson seldom leaves his cell in the city's Folsom Prison in case he is attacked by fellow inmates.

founded in Germany in 1902 and revived in England in 1911 by the notorious occultist Aleister Crowley. The Southern California branch of the O.T.O. was controlled by Mrs. Georgina Brayton, who used drugs and psychological pressure to forge its members into a hate force. One of their activities was to try to send hate vibrations into the black ghetto of Watts, hoping to start a riot. Like Manson they believed a racial war was imminent and made elaborate preparations to escape it by hiding out in the desert. And like the Kirké cult, they also sacrified animals.

Perhaps even more sinister was the Process Church of the Final Judgment, a cult formed in England in the mid-1960s under the malign leadership of two former Scientologists, Mary Anne and Robert DeGrimston. They quickly attracted a small but affluent following drawn mainly from the upper-class young—who were cheerfully invited to "dissipate their fortunes" by contributing lavishly to the Process—and from the entertainment world. The beliefs of the Process are a jumble of satanism, reincarnation (Mrs. DeGrimston at one point believed herself to be the reincarnation of Goebbels; her husband claims to be Christ), telepathy, and destruction. In one book, entitled *Satan on War*, Robert DeGrimston wrote: "Release the fiend that lies dormant within you, for he is strong and ruthless and his power is far beyond the bounds of human frailty." The Process worshiped three gods: Jehovah, Lucifer, and Satan. Christ was supposed to bring about the purification of all three. "Christ said love your enemy," said one Process publication. "Christ's enemy was Satan. Love Christ and Satan. . . . The Lamb and the Goat must come together. Pure love descended from the Pinnacle of Heaven, united with Pure Hatred raised from the depths of Hell." There was to be a Final Judgment, with Christ and Satan collaborating in the annihilation of the "Gray Forces" of moderation. These, according to an ex-Processan, included the "rich establishment" and the blacks.

This uplifting message was brought to California in 1967 by DeGrimston and some of his followers, accompanied by their pack of German Shepherd dogs. They set up a headquarters in the Haight-Ashbury district of San Francisco. Later, they recruited members in Los Angeles and New Orleans, and on the East Coast. For a while, Charles Manson and his then-small Family lived just two blocks away from the Process headquarters in San Francisco. Although there is no evidence that Manson ever belonged to the sect, he was visited while in prison by two representatives of the Process called "Father John" and "Brother Matthew." Moreover, the striking parallels between the Family's convoluted hate-love-violence credo and that of the Process suggest that Manson was possibly infected in some degree by their teachings.

After he was arrested for the Tate-LaBianca murders, Manson elicited a certain amount of support from the more deranged segments of the underground culture. One of the Weathermen, speaking at a Students for a Democratic Society convention, said: "Offing those rich pigs with their own forks and knives, and then eating a meal in the same room, far out! The Weathermen dig Charles Manson." The underground paper *Tuesday's Child*, "Voice of the Yippies," named Manson "Man of the Year."

Buttons urging "Free Manson" appeared in shops selling psychedelic items.

It is easy to become alarmed at this poisonous blossoming of cults dedicated to hatred and death and to conclude that violence is on the increase. Yet our society may be no more violent than those of other times and places. The violence is more efficiently publicized, however, and takes new forms. Throughout history there have been cults that provided expression for man's violent tendencies—in addition to the official outlets for violence, such as wars, religious persecutions, and witch hunts.

As long ago as 1200 B.C., and probably earlier, members of the cult of Dionysus, the Greek god of fruitfulness and wine, indulged in frenzied orgies that sometimes included tearing apart and consuming raw a sacrificial victim. The victim, representing the god, may in some cases have been human.

Very different in kind from the excesses of the Dionysus worshipers were the cold-blooded, disciplined murders carried out by the Assassins. This dedicated band of killers, formed in the 11th century, inspired terror in both Muslims and Christians. Medieval historians probably exaggerated the crimes of the Assassins, but there is no doubt that they were ruthless.

The Assassins were a product of the Shias, an unorthodox branch of the Muslim faith that had split away from the orthodox faith soon after Muhammad's death in A.D. 632 and that included a number of secret sects. Their *imams* (priest-kings) were the spiritual descendants of the Prophet's daughter Fatima and his son-in-law Ali. Despite persecution by orthodox Muslims, or

Above: Robert DeGrimston (left) with his wife Mary and other members of the Process Church of the Final Judgment. In 1967, the Process set up in San Francisco's Haight-Ashbury district, center of hippie culture. There, its jumbled message of Christianity and satanism may well have reached and influenced Charles Manson. Below: Jane Spielman, arrested for making bombs. Jane belonged to the Weathermen, a militant student group that supported Manson.

Above: Persian manuscript illustration showing (at the right) Hasan bin Sabbah, founder of the Assassins. Hasan's organization was an offshoot of the Ismaili Muslim sect, which challenged the right of the caliphs of Baghdad to rule the Muslim world. From his first fortress at Alamut, high in the northern mountains of Persia, Hasan founded other strongholds from which his followers could sally forth to raid or kill the ruling Turks. So successful were they that the word *assassin* has passed from Arabic into English and French to mean a political murderer.

Sunnis, the Shias survived, taking strength from their belief in the value of suffering for the sake of religion. In time, however, the Shias themselves split into two groups over a dispute regarding the line of succession to the throne of the imam. When the sixth imam died, he was succeeded by a younger son—the elder, Ismail, having been passed over. The Shias who supported Ismail and his descendants called themselves Ismailis. Although regarded as cranks by other Muslims, the Ismailis soon became an important branch of the faith. In Cairo, they established their own caliphate and founded a "hall of wisdom," where students not only acquired the academic knowledge of the times but also were indoctrinated with the secret teachings of the Ismaili faith.

The Ismailis worked secretly throughout the vast Islamic Empire to overthrow its ruler, the Sunni caliph of Baghdad. They had nearly succeeded in their conquest of Islam when the Turks (who were orthodox Muslims) gained control of large areas of the Islamic world.

Persia became one of the Turkish domains, and it was in Persia that the future chief of the Assassins was born. Hasan bin Sabbah was converted to Ismailism as a young man, and in 1067 he made the long journey to Cairo, where he spent three years in the caliph's court. Then he returned to Persia to spread the Ismaili faith by militant means.

After gaining a substantial number of converts—partly by appealing to the natives' hatred of the Turks, whom he promised to drive out of Persia—Hasan established a stronghold. This was the fortress of Alamut (or Eagle's Nest), which Hasan and his followers infiltrated and captured with remarkably little op-

position. From this castle, perched in the mountains dominating a 30-mile-long valley, Hasan operated a profitable protection racket, launched campaigns of missionary activity and subversion, and sent forth his dedicated political assassins.

The name *assassin* is derived from the Arabic word *Hashshashin*, which means "users of hashish." It is possible that the unquestioning obedience of Hasan's killers was due to their being drugged. But one writer has suggested that the Assassins acquired their name merely through a resemblance to drug-crazed people.

One of the many legends surrounding the Assassins is that young men trained in the use of weapons were drugged and then taken to a beautiful garden near the castle. When they regained consciousness they found themselves surrounded by exquisite flowers and fruit trees, splashing fountains, and gilded pavilions. Beautiful girls, practiced in the art of love as well as music and dancing, gratified the desires of the bedazzled young men. After several days of living in luxury, the recruits were drugged again and returned to Hasan's court, which, by contrast, was extremely puritanical. Here they were told that they had had a foretaste of paradise, to which they would immediately be sent if they died as a result of performing a service for their chief.

Whether or not the paradise garden story is true, the Assassins were thoroughly indoctrinated with the Ismaili belief that there was no good or evil except the virtue of obeying the imam, whose representative Hasan was. A visitor to Alamut recorded an incident typical of those repeated in many European chronicles. He was standing on the ramparts of the castle with Hasan, when Hasan pointed out to him a white-robed guard standing on a

Above: the castle of Masyaf, near Hama in Syria, one of the principal Assassin fortresses. Below: Hasan pours drugged wine for Assassin initiates. The name *assassin* derives from the Arabic *Hashshashin*, meaning "users of hashish." It is not known whether the drug was used only to ensure obedience, or whether the Assassins killed while under its influence.

nearby parapet. "You see that devotee standing guard on yonder turret-top?" said Hasan. "Watch!" He made a signal to the man, who instantly threw up his hands in salutation and plunged 2000 feet to his death.

Most of the deaths ordered by Hasan were not capricious but matters of strategy. He lacked the numbers to wage all-out war upon the Turks, but he could pick off their leaders and Arab allies singly and so undermine their strength.

His first victim was Nizam Al-Mulk, Vizier to the Turkish Sultan. According to legend, Hasan and Nizam and the poet Omar Khayyam had been schoolmates. In adulthood, so the story goes, Nizam had given Hasan a position at the Sultan's court; then, sensing his friend's increasing power, he had brought about his downfall. Thus, personal vengeance may have formed part of Hasan's determination to kill Nizam.

A volunteer, Bu Tahir Arrani, disguised himself as a Sufi, or holy man, and approached Nizam when he was being carried on a litter from his audience tent, ostensibly to beg a favor. He pulled a dagger from inside his robe and stabbed Nizam in the chest. Immediately, he himself was killed by the Vizier's guards.

During the next 30 years, Hasan's minions infiltrated, intimidated, and often assassinated his enemies, both political and religious. Eventually, no person in authority would venture out without wearing armor under his robes. The killers dispatched their victims openly, in a mosque or a public street, and were often killed themselves immediately afterward.

Despite Hasan's cunning strategy, he ultimately failed to

Below: the murder of Nizam Al-Mulk, first victim of the Assassins. Nizam was Vizier to the Turkish Sultan and one of the leaders of the Sunni Muslims. His murder was therefore of great political importance to Hasan bin Sabbah and the Ismaili sect.

Above: King Louis IX of France receives envoys from the leader of the Assassins during the Sixth Crusade. According to Joinville's *Chronicle*, written in the 13th century, Louis answered the envoys' threats by threatening the Assassin leader in his turn, and an alliance was subsequently formed between the Assassins and the crusading king of France.

Right: the siege of Alamut by the Mongols in 1256. Alamut and the other Assassin fortresses eventually surrendered to the invaders, in the hope of escaping the ghastly treatment the barbarians meted out to those they vanquished. But their surrender did not prevent the Mongols from massacring the Persian Ismailis and so, with the Mongol invasion, the rule of the Assassins was brought to an end.

achieve his aims. The Turks remained in power in Persia; and the Cairo caliphate fell into the hands of the party opposed to him. Hasan, the "Old Man of the Mountain," died at the age of 90. His policies were continued by his first two successors, but by the mid-12th century the Persian Ismailis had returned to a more orthodox form of Islam. The Syrian "mission" of Assassins, established by Hasan, turned to killing for cash. By siding now with the Sultan Saladin and now with the Crusaders, the Syrian Assassins preserved their independence and power, and gained a reputation for ruthlessness that lived in European history for many centuries.

More mysterious and sinister than the Assassins—whose motives were at least comprehensible—were the Thugs of India. Members of this secret sect killed to serve their goddess Kali, the Hindu goddess of death, who according to legend had entrusted them with killing the demons that threatened the earth. By some

Above: a party of Thugs prepares to murder a traveler. Two *sothas*, or deceivers, divert the man's attention, while the *bhartote* or strangler prepares the knotted *rumal* or waistcloth with which all Thuggee murders were carried out. Until the middle of the 19th century, an Indian traveler was in as great danger from the Thugs as from the other perils of the road, and it is estimated that tens of thousands of travelers were ritually murdered by the sect every year.

obscure line of reasoning, the demons became identified in the minds of the Thugs with travelers. Every year during the pilgrimage season, thousands of travelers would be murdered as they made their way over the roads of India. A pilgrim's disappearance was seldom investigated by his relatives, for in a land infested with cobras, cholera, and ordinary bandits, as well as Thugs, it was not surprising if someone failed to return home.

Thuggee originated in the Middle Ages. Although dedicated to a Hindu goddess, the sect consisted mainly of Muslims, and some writers think it may have some connection with the Assassins. But the secrecy and cunning with which the Thugs practiced their vocation contrast sharply with the open and suicidal methods of the followers of Hasan.

The Thugs were also called *Phansigars*, a name derived from the Hindustani word for "noose," for it was by strangling that they dispatched their victims. The murder weapon was a *rumal* (scarf) that they wore tied around their waists. The procedure was carefully worked out and efficient. Bands of Thugs would lie in wait along the pilgrimage routes. Two or three of them would strike up an acquaintance with a pilgrim—usually a rich one— and accompany him on his way. They would leave signs along the road for their confederates, letting them know that they had obtained a victim. Gradually, other members of the gang would attach themselves to the little group. At an agreed signal, one of the Thugs would slip his rumal around the victim's neck, and with the aid of another Thug draw it tight. Meanwhile, a third man would seize the victim's legs and pull them backward, thus throwing him face downward on the ground so that he could offer little resistance.

Thugs sometimes attached themselves to parties of pilgrims

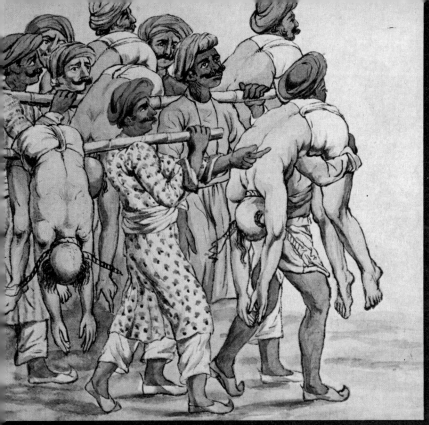

Left: Thugs carry the bodies of their victims away from the murder site to be buried. It was often several years before the disappearance of a victim of Thuggee was noticed, so great were the distances to be traveled in India. Even after it was quite certain that a traveler had vanished on the journey, his death was usually ascribed to wild beasts, snakes, or disease, rather than to the work of Thugs. Below: Thug murderers stab the eyes and bodies of the travelers they have killed. The ritual aspect of Thuggee demanded that the corpses of all the sect's victims should be mutilated before being buried or—as in this case—thrown down a well. After the bodies had been disposed of, the Thugs held a ritual feast of *Tuponee*, often on the site of the newly made grave.

and killed all of them. After such a killing they would dismember the bodies and disfigure the faces, partly as a practical step to prevent identification of the victims and partly as a service to Kali. Each band included one ritual butcher for this purpose. The Thugs would then dig a grave for the mutilated corpses, with the help of their pickaxes, which they considered sacred symbols of their calling. After burying their victims the Thugs would sometimes camp or feast over the grave to obliterate traces of newly dug earth.

The *Tuponee* (ritual feast) that followed every Thug killing reinforced the initiates' sense of sacred mission. A tent was erected and a cloth spread on the ground. The leader of the gang sat on the cloth, surrounded by some of the most experienced stranglers. Thugs of lower ranks sat outside the circle. Before

Below: Thugs turned carpet weavers, photographed in Jubbulpore
in 1874 with one of their products. Thug carpets became so famous
that Queen Victoria ordered one, which can still be seen in the
Waterloo Chamber of Windsor Castle. William Sleeman, who was
responsible for the suppression of Thuggee, founded schools to teach
the sons of Thugs such trades as weaving, brickmaking, or building.

the leader on the cloth lay the consecrated pickax and a piece
of silver, a symbolic offering to Kali, and some *goor* (coarse
sugar), which they regarded as holy food. The leader would dig a
small hole in the earth and pour in some of the goor, while re-
citing a prayer to Kali. He would then sprinkle holy water on the
pit containing the goor and on the pickax, while the other Thugs
repeated the prayer. Goor was distributed to those who had
proved themselves by killing. If a novice happened to take any,
he was forced to go out at once and strangle someone.

This feast had a profound effect on the participants. A Thug
leader named Feringheea told his British captors: "We all feel
pity sometimes, but the goor of the Tuponee changes our nature.
It would change the nature of a horse. Let any man taste of that
goor, and he will be a Thug though he know all the trades and
have all the wealth in the world. I never wanted food; my mother's
family was opulent, her relations high in office. I have been high
in office myself . . . yet I was always miserable while absent from
my gang, and obliged to return to Thuggee. My father made me
taste of that fatal goor when I was a mere boy; and if I were to
live a thousand years I should never be able to follow any other
trade."

"Fatal" was a key word in the Thugs' mentality. They believed
that it was their destiny to kill for Kali and that their victims
were preordained to die. Apart from their gory business during
the pilgrimage season, Thugs pursued peaceful, often exemplary,
lives. *Thug*, in fact, means "one who deceives," a reference to
their façade of virtue. One Thug served as a devoted nurse to a
family of British children—except for the few weeks every year
when he went off to visit his "sick mother."

Left: the ritual Thug murder. While the bhartote tightens the rumal around his victim's neck, his accomplices hold the man's hands and feet. Traditionally, as soon as the noose was placed around the victim's neck he was thrown forward face down onto the ground. In this position he was helpless, unable to offer any resistance to his murderers.

Above: the Prince of Wales, later King Edward VII of Britain, is entertained during his tour of India in 1877 by a demonstration of the Thugs' strangling technique. By this time, the vigilance of the British, combined with vastly improved communications, had wiped out Thuggee as a living cult. The men giving this demonstration are former Thugs, who had been jailed for their membership of the sect.

In its early days, the sect established certain restrictions to their killing. As Kali was a woman, they would spare women. They also spared lepers, the blind or mutilated, and anyone driving a cow or female goat. Craftsmen whose work was protected by Kali—gold-, iron-, and brass-workers, smiths, carpenters, stonecutters, and shoemakers—could travel unmolested.

Occasionally, a gang would violate this code, and any subsequent disaster that befell the gang would be attributed to their misdeed. By the time British rule was established in India during the 18th century such violations were fairly common. When the government launched a campaign to eradicate Thuggee, and began capturing, trying, and executing its members, many Thugs believed that the breaking of their own taboos had brought about their misfortunes.

The British granted pardons to those Thugs who supplied them with valuable information. Most Thugs who were tried were either transported or imprisoned for life, and only 466 of the 3689 Thugs tried before 1840 were hanged. By the middle of the 19th century, Thuggee was no longer a threat. Occasional outbreaks have been reported since then—some as recently as the 1940s—but although Kali still has her devotees, her death cult is virtually extinct.

Few cults in the history of the world have practiced violence with the degree of ritual and refinement developed by the Thugs. Few have killed with such conviction that the killing itself was a sacred act. But many cults have resorted to violence as a way of asserting or gaining power, getting revenge upon society (as Manson's Family did), or determining the structure of power within the group.

41

3

Cults and Politics

Originally they called themselves the Poor Fellow-Soldiers of Christ and the Temple of Solomon. They were a small band of knights who had conceived the plan of protecting pilgrims to the Holy Land. The success of the First Crusade in 1099 had opened up Jerusalem and other sacred places to European travelers, but the route was fraught with dangers. Saracen bandits lay in wait at certain ambush points to separate pilgrims from their money and sometimes from their lives as well.

One Hugh de Payens, a veteran of the First Crusade, decided, along with another knight, to hide at one of these ambush points

Above: the Grand Master of the Knights Templars. The Templars, a religious Order of knights founded to protect pilgrims in the Holy Land, took vows of poverty, chastity, and obedience in much the same way as monks. In time, however, the Order grew so rich and powerful that it wielded considerable political force.

Right: the "tracing board" of the third degree of Freemasonry, symbolic of the ceremony by which an apprentice is admitted as a Master Mason or full member of the craft. Freemasonry is not directly a political organization, but its liberal ideals have sometimes influenced political thought.

"Their investitures were held at night, in a guarded chapter house"

and surprise the bandits in the act of attacking. From this successful and satisfying escapade grew the idea of forming a group dedicated to the protection of pilgrims. Soon Hugh de Payens and his little band of knights organized themselves as a religious Order. They took an oath to the Patriarch (bishop) of Jerusalem to guard the public roads, to forsake worldly chivalry, to live in chastity, obedience, and poverty, and "to fight with a pure mind for the supreme and true King."

Recognizing the potential usefulness of this group of Christian soldiers, King Baldwin II of Jerusalem gave them a part of the royal palace that stood next to the site of Solomon's Temple. This was the first of many such gifts the Templars received throughout the next 200 years. Eventually they would become one of the most powerful forces in Europe, and their very power would bring about their destruction.

In the beginning, however, they were noted mainly for their piety, bravery, and disdain of material comforts. They took pride in never changing their mantles until the fabric rotted or was slashed by enemy swords. "You see them never combed," wrote St. Bernard of Clairvaux approvingly, contrasting them with rich, well-accoutered knights, "rarely washed, their beards bushy, sweaty, dusty, stained by their harness and the heat." St. Bernard, founder of the strict Cistercian Order of monks, was an early and powerful patron of the Templars. He commended their practice of seeking out excommunicated knights and converting them to the devout and disciplined life of their Order. He sent Hugh de Payens, the Grand Master, a letter praising the work of the Templars in rehabilitating the assorted "rogues and impious men, robbers and committers of sacrilege, murderers, perjurers, and adulterers" who found their way to the Holy Land. With this encouragement from one of the most influential men of his time, Hugh set off for the Council of Troyes, a high-level meeting of clergy and important laity, to secure recognition for his Order in Europe. There, under the sponsorship of Bernard, he submitted the Rule of his brotherhood, called the Rule of the Temple, which followed to some extent the Cistercian Rule. It covered every aspect of the Templars' organization, way of life, duties and privileges, and rituals. The copies of the Rule existing today are incomplete; and the complete Rule was known only to the highest officers. To weld a group of adventurers into a unified, dedicated force, the founders realized that a certain amount of secret ceremony, unique to their Order, would be necessary. Their investitures were held at night, in a guarded chapter house. This secrecy—and the widespread belief among outsiders during the Order's last years that the secrecy cloaked lewd and blasphemous practices—was one cause of their undoing.

In 1128, however, the fledgling Order received nothing but acclaim and gifts. Sanctioned by the Council of Troyes, and its members now exempted from excommunication, it went from strength to strength. Everywhere Hugh went in Europe, kings and nobles outdid each other in contributing to the Order. Forest lands, farms, castles, whole villages came their way, as did a miscellany of practical smaller gifts: a suit of armor, a horse, an annual supply of one shirt and one pair of drawers.

Left: *The Battle between Baldwin and the Turks.* This French painting depicts an episode in the Crusades, the holy wars fought to free Jerusalem and the holy places of Christianity from Muslim rule. After the First Crusade had opened Palestine to Christian travelers, the Order of Knights Templars was founded by Hugh de Payens to protect pilgrims there. Below: 15th-century painting of Jerusalem, holy city of Christianity and goal of the Crusaders.

Left: St. Bernard giving the Knights Templars their Rule. St. Bernard, Abbot of Clairvaux in France, was one of the first patrons of the Templars and on the basis of his recommendation Hugh de Payens was able to obtain papal sanction for the Order. The "Rule" shown here contained not only the regulations governing the Templars' life, but also their secret initiation rites.

45

Some years later, the Church granted the Templars the right to have their own churches and clergy; they were exempt from tithes (as well as from secular taxes); they were subservient to the Pope alone. Their independence, however, did not go unchallenged. Bishops and parish priests resented the Templars' power, and disputes between the two camps were frequent. But the papacy—dedicated as it was to strengthening the Christian presence in the Holy Land—stood solidly behind the Templars and issued one decree after another to protect them. In fact, anyone who persecuted the Templars was liable to excommunication.

In the disastrous Second Crusade, from 1146 to 1150, the Templars repaid the confidence placed in them by fighting valiantly and preventing the total catastrophe this misguided campaign might otherwise have been. The secretary to Louis VII of France praised their discipline and obedience to their Grand Master: "All . . . gave the word that they would not flee the field, and that they would obey in everything the Master who was given to them." King Louis, also, acknowledged his dependence on the

Above: Krak de Chevaliers, a Templar fortress in Syria. In the Middle Ages, religious orders often received large gifts of money and the Templars grew wealthy enough to maintain huge castles such as Krak—and to act as bankers to the Middle East and later to the European courts. Although early leaders remained true to their pious vows, later Grand Masters used the power this wealth gave them to further their own ambitious ends. Left: Jacques de Molay is received into the Templars. The secrecy of the Templars' initiation rites led to accusations of blasphemy and obscenity.

Templars: "We could not imagine," he wrote, "how We could have lasted a moment in this country without their aid and assistance. Their help was available from the first day of Our arrival until the moment We send this letter."

In the years that followed, the Templars fought in many battles, some of their own instigation. Not all the later Grand Masters were so altruistic and pious as Hugh de Payens. The convoluted politics of the Holy Land, where rival groups within both Christian and Muslim camps maneuvered for control, offered plenty of opportunities for the Templars to gain power and to influence the course of events. They rode under banners proclaiming in Latin, "Not to ourselves, Lord, not to ourselves, but to Thy name give the glory." Nevertheless, as an almost autonomous community within Christendom and as a rich landowner (with an annual income in Europe alone of $90 million), the Templars enjoyed much of the glory of this world.

A large part of their power derived from their position as the main bankers in Europe and the Middle East. With their scattered and well-fortified castles they were ideally placed to

Above: one of the Templars arrested in 1307 kneels at the feet of the Pope, Clement V, and King Philip IV of France. It was Philip, jealous of the power and wealth of the Templars, who brought about the destruction of the Order, aided, albeit somewhat unwillingly, by Pope Clement. One October night in 1307, Philip had about 15,000 Templars and Templar servants arrested, and many of these were later tortured to obtain "confessions." In their agony, the tortured admitted that their rites contained blasphemous and obscene acts, and that they worshiped the Devil—sufficient evidence, according to Philip, for the Order to be suppressed.

47

Above: stone carving of Baphomet, one of the demons the Knights Templars were accused of worshiping. The name Baphomet is in fact a corruption of Muhammad, prophet of the Islamic faith.
Below: Jacques de Molay, his hands bound after his arrest. De Molay was the last Grand Master of the Templars, being head of the Order when Philip began his campaign of persecution. Like so many of his followers, de Molay was unable to remain true to his vows under torture, and he admitted every charge Philip wished.

guard and transport money, and their religious status promised integrity. During truces they even did business with the Muslims, who thought it prudent to have some money invested with the Christians in case the fortunes of war should lead them into a European alliance. The kings of England, France, and other European countries deposited their treasure with the Templars and on occasion borrowed from them.

It was one of their royal debtors, Philip IV of France—called "the Fair," for his good looks, not for his sense of justice—who brought about the destruction of the Order, aided by Pope Clement V. By this time—the beginning of the 14th century—the Christians had lost their holdings in Palestine, and the Templars' headquarters were moved to Cyprus. In Europe, however, the Order remained enormously powerful. Philip, who was in a financial crisis of his own making, resolved to break their power and appropriate their wealth. He favored a scheme to merge them with the Hospitaler Knights as a single Order, the "Knights of Jerusalem," whose Grand Master would always be a prince of the royal house of France. But this plan was opposed by both Templars and Hospitalers. Philip's chance came in the form of an ex-Templar named Esquiu de Florian, who brought him lurid stories of blasphemy, sexual perversion, and Devil worship in the Order. Initiates, he said, were required to spit on the crucifix and to kiss the mouth, navel, and anus of their initiator. They practiced sodomy and they worshiped the Devil.

These charges were just what Philip wanted to hear. He planted some spies in the Order to gather evidence, and in the meantime tried to enlist the support of Clement V, who owed his triple crown to Philip's assistance. The Pope hesitated. "There is so much that still appears impossible to credit," he wrote to the king. "However, since we attach great weight to your communications in this matter. . . ." He did not, in so many words, forbid an indictment of the Templars, and Philip took action. On the night of October 12, 1307, his officers throughout France arrested some 15,000 people, including not only Templars, but also the artisans and laborers on their estates. The Grand Master, Jacques de Molay, then in Paris, was among those arrested.

The Templars were interrogated by the Inquisition and tortured by Philip's officials in an effort to obtain as many confessions as possible. Not surprisingly, these methods were quite successful. Of the 138 Templars interrogated in Paris during the first month, 123 confessed to spitting on, or "near," the crucifix during their initiation. Many of them confessed to the other charges, though in regard to the Devil worship the details conflicted somewhat. They admitted that in secret ceremonies they worshiped a kind of idol, but whether this was a human skull encrusted with jewels, or the remains of a former Grand Master, or a head with three faces, or a representation of Baphomet (a corruption of "Muhammad" and the medieval term for a foreign god, or "devil") remained a matter for conjecture. No idol answering any of these descriptions was ever found during the search of the Templars' domains in France. As for the cat that supposedly represented the Devil in other secret rituals, it was variously reported as gray, black, ginger, and gray tabby. Modern writers on the subject generally agree that blasphemy may have played some part in the Templars' initiations—perhaps as a test of obedience. And some homosexual practices, in a membership of 20,000 men denied female company, would hardly be surprising. The other charges appear to have been fabrications.

Those Templars who did not die under torture were required to confirm their confessions voluntarily three days later. Those who reiterated their confessions were given penance and/or prison sentences, depending on the crime; those who recanted were treated as heretics and handed to the state for execution.

During the seven years following the arrest of the Templars in France, the once proud and powerful Order became something of a political football. The vacillating Pope asserted his authority and took the prosecution of the Order into his own hands—first suspending the powers of the Inquisition in France, then issuing a bull calling all kings and princes to arrest the Templars, then disputing with Philip the procedure to be followed in bringing the Order to trial.

After considerable delay and pre-trial investigations by the Church, the public trial of the Templars began in April 1310, in the town of Vienne in southern France. Many Templars recanted

Above: Jacques de Molay and other leading Templars are burned to death at the stake. When de Molay was led out for sentencing, he retracted his "confession," asserting that it was only torture that had made him admit his guilt. According to legend, as the flames crept around de Molay's body he pointed at King Philip, who was attending the execution, and cursed him, his minister Nogaret, and Pope Clement, prophesying the deaths of all three within a year.

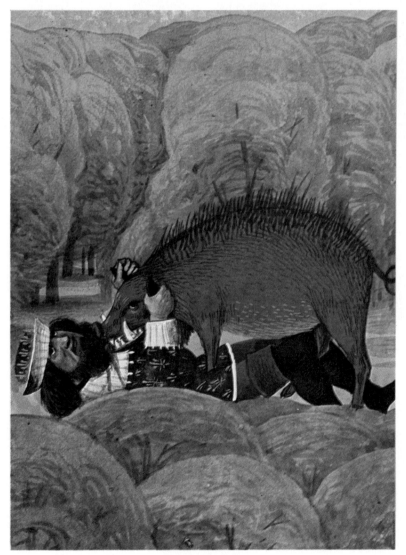

Left: the death of King Philip, from a 15th-century manuscript. Philip died suddenly during a hunting expedition, about eight months after de Molay's death. By that time, Pope Clement was already dead and soon afterward Nogaret too had met his fate. Were their deaths simply coincidence, or had they been struck down by de Molay's curse?

Left: George Washington as a Freemason. Washington was Grand Master of his Masonic lodge when he became the first President of the United States in 1789. Throughout history, the ideals of freedom and liberty preached by the Freemasons have attracted eminent and powerful men to the order—in Britain the movement traditionally has a close connection with the Royal Family and the present Grand Master of England is the Duke of Kent. Denis Diderot, the 18th-century French philosopher, was a Freemason and Masonic ideals may have influenced those responsible for the French Revolution of 1789.

their previous confessions to defend their Order; 67 of these were then burned at the stake as relapsed heretics. Thus discouraged, the Templars refrained from defending themselves. The trial dragged on. Two years after it had begun the Pope issued a bull proclaiming the dissolution of the Templars. He admitted that the evidence—mainly hearsay and enforced confessions—was inadequate to convict them. But he, the Holy Father, was convinced of their guilt and that should be enough.

Most of the Templars who had confessed and maintained their confessions were set free. Four of the top-ranking officers, including the Grand Master, who had recanted their original confessions now confessed again. They were sentenced to life imprisonment. The sentence of these four was pronounced in

Left: 19th-century French illustration of the initiation of a Freemason. Traditional—and supposedly secret—rituals are used for every Masonic ceremony. Below: reconstruction of the beginning of the ceremony whereby a new Mason is initiated into the craft. The candidate, blindfolded and in traditional garb, is halted at the door by the Inner Guard, who holds a dagger to his bared breast. The form of dress and the blue aprons used in English Masonic lodges today are very like those worn by the 19th-century French Masons in the picture on the left—as is the candidate's initiation attire.

public in front of the Cathedral of Notre Dame in Paris. Then came the surprise. Jacques de Molay addressed the crowd: "I confess that I am indeed guilty of the greatest infamy. But the infamy is that I have lied . . . in admitting the disgusting charges laid against my Order. I declare . . . that the Order is innocent. Its purity and saintliness have never been defiled. In truth, I had testified otherwise, but I did so from fear of terrible tortures. . . . Life is offered me, but at the price of perfidy. At such a price life is not worth having."

One of his companions, Geoffrey de Charnay, also declared the Order's innocence. Their speeches caused a furor among the crowd, now sympathetic to the Templars, and before things could get out of hand, the authorities took the four prisoners away.

Once more, the Crown took charge. Philip took control of the two stubborn knights and on the following morning, March 19, 1314, they were burned at the stake, still protesting their innocence. Philip watched. As the flames enveloped Jacques de Molay's body, he turned his head toward the royal party and cried: "Pope Clement, Chevalier Guillaume de Nogaret, King Philip, I summon you to the tribunal of Heaven before the year is out, to receive your just punishment! Accursed! Accursed! You shall be accursed to the thirteenth generation of your lines!"

Almost exactly a month later, Pope Clement died. Philip followed him in November of that same year, during a hunting expedition. His Minister, Nogaret, who had played a leading role in the Templars' destruction, died a few weeks later, under mysterious circumstances.

The Templars' clash with the state—and with the Church acting in the interests of the state—was a direct result of their power and wealth. They seem to have had no political aims or desire to change society at large. By contrast, the conflict four

Left: cartoon taken from an 1884 edition of the American magazine *Puck*, satirizing the conflict between the Freemasons and the Roman Catholic Church. Pope after Pope issued encyclicals denouncing Freemasonry, and the latest of these appeared in 1884. Although supposedly binding on Roman Catholics everywhere, the Papal condemnation did not prevent Catholics from remaining—and indeed, becoming—Masons. In this cartoon, the Masonic protagonist is depicted with one shoe removed, a satire on the required mode of dress at Masonic initiation ceremonies, which has often caused non-Masons considerable amusement.

Above: title page of *The Mysteries of Freemasonry*, a fictitious exposé of the "true" purposes of the sect by Frenchman Léo Taxil. Taxil accused the Masons of Devil worship and other forms of debauchery, and in this drawing a Masonic lodge is worshiping the demon Baphomet, a supposed god of the Order of Knights Templars.

centuries later between the Freemasons and established authority was political in its essence. The Masons had certain political ideas that some rulers were not prepared to tolerate.

Freemasonry as we know it today is an outgrowth of the medieval craft guilds of practicing masons. In the Middle Ages, a mason—particularly one who carved in freestone, the kind used for arches and decoration, as opposed to blocks—enjoyed some prestige. Such men were also called *freemasons* because they were free to move where they liked, free of restrictions from feudal lord or town council. In their guilds, called *lodges*, they preserved secrets of the trade, and established ethical codes for themselves. They also had secret signs of recognition to prevent outsiders infiltrating their ranks.

By the 17th century, in Britain, the masons were accepting honorary members—gentlemen who had an interest in architecture (a profession that grew out of the craft of mason), or who were attracted to the secret aspects of freemasonry. In time, a distinct non-practicing or "speculative" form of Freemasonry came into being. The materials, tools, and methods of practicing masons were endowed with symbolic meaning, some of it relating to the building of Solomon's Temple, considered an allegory of the perfection of the individual.

In Britain, Freemasonry was highly respectable, and it has always included some eminent people including members of the Royal Family. In the American Colonies, leaders of the Revolutionary cause, including George Washington, Benjamin Franklin, and Alexander Hamilton, were Masons. Principles cherished by Masons (and, of course, by other enlightened men of the 18th century), such as freedom of speech and of the press, freedom of worship, representative government, and freedom from arbitrary arrest, were incorporated in the new American Constitution.

On the Continent, Freemasonry had a more turbulent existence. Although some monarchs tolerated the movement—and some, such as Frederick the Great of Prussia, even joined it—others rightly suspected that its liberal ideas were a threat to their power and did their best to suppress it. It also quickly came into conflict with the Roman Catholic Church. In 1738, some 20 years after its establishment on the Continent, Freemasonry was denounced by Pope Clement XII, who forbade Catholics to become members on pain of excommunication. He maintained that Masons must have something to hide; otherwise they would not insist on secrecy. They were, he thought, "depraved and perverted," dangerous to "the well-being of souls," and "most suspect of heresy." Some Catholic countries, such as France and Austria, simply ignored Clement's bull; but in Spain and Portugal it was accepted, and there Freemasons were arrested and tortured by the Inquisition.

Ironically, for a brief period early in the 18th century there was an alliance between Jesuits and Freemasons—specifically, a small group of Scottish Jacobites (supporters of the exiled Stuart monarch) living in France. A Scotsman named Michael Ramsay introduced a new system of Masonic rites—he claimed they were old Scottish rites—into the French lodges, with the purpose of arousing sympathy and assistance for the Jacobite cause. The

Below: coronation of the queen of the Daughters of the Nile in Omaha, Nebraska in 1956. The Daughters of the Nile is an organization of the wives of members of the Shriner sect, a quasi-Masonic group whose purpose is philanthropic. A number of such offshoots of Freemasonry as the Shriners now exist in the United States; few of them maintain the essential secrecy of Freemasonry, and most replace Freemasonry's religious element by such dramatic ritual as this.

Jesuits, traditional supporters of the Catholic Stuarts, also supported the "Scottish" Masons. As for the Stuart Pretender himself, he dismissed Ramsay as a madman.

Throughout its history, Freemasonry had been suspected of being behind all sorts of political upheavals: the French Revolution, the Russian Revolution, the Spanish Civil War, and the assassination of Archduke Franz Ferdinand in 1914, which precipitated World War I. The supposed existence of a worldwide conspiracy of Masons—often linked with a supposed conspiracy of Jews—bent on undermining the established order in some way has been a cherished myth among certain demagogues. Both Hitler and Mussolini persecuted the Masons, and many of them died in concentration camps.

Certainly Masons have participated in some political movements. The Carbonari, a secret society in the 1800s engaged in the unification of Italy, was composed mainly of Masons, and the society's liberal philosophy closely paralleled Masonic beliefs.

Earlier, Masonic influence had been detected in the French Revolution of 1789–92, with some writers claiming that those shattering events were engineered by a small group of 27 Masons. Such an idea is generally discredited by modern historians, but it is true that some of the writers whose ideas informed the Revolution, in its early stages at least, were also Masons: Diderot was one, and so, probably, was Voltaire. But the notion that the leaders of the Revolution were Masons, or were even sympathetic to Masons, is untrue: once in power they outlawed the society.

The Revolution spawned a number of cults, none of which lasted more than a few years. First of all there was the official cult of "Reason," which became for a while the official religion. Churches throughout France were converted into temples of Reason, in which appropriate ceremonies supplanted the celebration of the Mass. In his book *Religious History of Modern France*, Adrien Dansette describes one of these rituals: "A rock was placed in the choir of Notre Dame and on it a circular temple was erected, dedicated to 'philosophy.' On the morning of the 10th November, in the presence of members of the Commune, a procession of girls marched up and down the sides of the rock, saluting as they passed the Flame of Truth which burned half way up. An actress from the Opéra, dressed in white and wearing an azure cloak and red bonnet, came out of the temple and seated herself on a grass-covered throne. She was Reason and the girls chanted a hymn to her. Then, with the goddess borne on the shoulders of four citizens, the participants and spectators set off for the Convention. . . ." The cult of Reason lasted only a few years; Napoleon reinstated the Roman Catholic Church.

The opposition, too, had its cults. These centered on the lost Dauphin, son of King Louis XVI, who had presumably died or been murdered in prison during the Terror. Even today, there are people who maintain that the Dauphin was not killed but escaped—some say to America. In the few decades following the Revolution, stories that Louis XVII was alive were widely circulated among monarchists, and various would-be kings tried to pass themselves off as the missing Dauphin. They found willing supporters among several cults dedicated to restoring the direct line of Louis XVI. One of these groups was the Johannites, who

Right: *Fête Républicaine, 1795*, an illustration of a festival of the cult of Reason, official "religion" of France after the French Revolution. Attempts by the revolutionary leaders to make the Church in France subordinate to the state had led to a break between Church and state, followed later by a partial "de-Christianization" of the country. Churches were converted into temples of Reason, dedicated to philosophy, to liberty, or to reason itself, and secular statues, like that of Reason in this picture, replaced images of the Virgin Mary and the saints.

Right: revolutionary French painting of 1791 entitled *The Civic Oath of the Bishops*. The revolutionary leaders' first step toward secularizing the clergy had been to make bishops and priests subject to election by property owners, rather than appointment by Church authorities as hitherto. The distaste with which this suggestion was viewed by many Churchmen was followed by a requirement that all priests should take an oath of loyalty to the Revolution. The Pope condemned the measure, and many of the clergy refused to take such an oath. With the priesthood viewed as the enemy of the state, religion lost ground in France, and the cult of Reason took hold.

had come into existence in 1772, when John the Baptist had supposedly appeared to a man named Loiseaut and prophesied blood, thunder, and the beheading of kings. This would be followed by a golden age, in which a "God-given prince" would rule the people. After the carnage of the Revolution had fulfilled the first prophecy, the Johannites awaited the realization of the second, and unsuccessfully sponsored seven or eight Pretenders.

Another vision, of a man in a yellow overcoat and tall hat, appeared in 1816 to a farmer named Thomas Martin, who was working in a field. The mysterious stranger told Martin to warn the present king, Louis XVIII, the brother of Louis XVI, that his life was in danger. Then the figure levitated and vanished. After several more visits from the stranger, Martin became convinced of the urgency of the message. He went to Paris, where he told his story to several highly placed officials. One of them decided to have Martin confined in the lunatic asylum in Charenton.

Eventually, Martin was released and was granted an interview with Louis XVIII, to whom he delivered his warning. By this time, the seer had attracted the attention of Dauphin supporters, including a group calling themselves the Saviors of Louis XVIII, who implanted in Martin's head the idea that his visions heralded the reappearance of the true king of France. He was feted by the aristocracy and considered a Divine spokesman.

In 1833, there arrived on the scene Karl Wilhelm Naundorff, a Berlin watchmaker who spoke no French but who claimed to be Louis XVII. He found plenty of people ready to accept his claim, and the prophet Martin, on being introduced to Naundorff, identified him as the king who had been revealed to him in a dream. Within the year Martin died; but Naundorff carried on as his own prophet, seeing visions, performing cures, and winning adherents to his cause. His attempt in 1836 to prove his case in court resulted in his imprisonment and exile to England.

A Pretender with a more democratic touch was Jean Simon Ganneau, who believed that he was Louis XVII returned to earth and that his wife was Marie Antoinette (a mother-to-wife transformation that would have delighted a Freudian analyst, had one been around). Ganneau also called himself the Mapah—a fusion of "Maman" and "Papa"—and his God was all humanity, Eve and Adam, also known as the "Evadah." Pronouncements from the Mapah mainly concerned the brotherhood of man, and despite his supposed Bourbon connections, he was an ardent revolutionary and took an active part in the 1848 Revolution.

A characteristic of most cults is the tendency to make members feel distinct from—and usually superior to—humanity at large. In Germany, in the first part of this century, a particularly unpleasant form of this exclusiveness flourished briefly. Several cults sprang up that were grouped together under the name *Völkischen*, a word referring to "the people" in a folkloric sense. They were an outgrowth of the 19th-century artistic and philosophical trend in Germany that glorified the history and mythology of the German people. Some of the Völkischen tried to revive pagan, Teutonic religions, particularly the worship of the god Wotan. Among themselves they supplanted Christian festivals with others commemorating German myths and historical events. They had their own wedding and baptism ceremonies, in which

Above: Karl Wilhelm Naundorff, a Berlin watchmaker who arrived in Paris in 1833 claiming to be the lost Dauphin (crown prince) of France. Although the Dauphin had been imprisoned during the Revolution with his parents, King Louis XVI and Queen Marie Antoinette, who were later guillotined, no concrete evidence of his death was ever found. Many of the political cults of post-Revolutionary France centered on the return of a supposed "Dauphin" to claim the throne.

Left: portrait of a young boy, presumed to be the Dauphin, Louis XVII of France. The Dauphin cults were based on the theory that the Dauphin had somehow managed to escape from prison and had then managed to live in hiding until the French Revolution came to an end.

Left: the German gods at the ordering of the world. The German Völkischen cults of the early 20th century hoped, by returning to the traditional German virtues and by eliminating foreign—principally Jewish—influences, to restore the essential purity of the Germanic master race.

Below: Poster portrait of Adolf Hitler, leader of Nazi Germany. Through slogans like this—proclaiming "One people, one empire, one leader!"—Nazi propaganda made Hitler into a godlike cult figure; his portrait replaced religious pictures in many Nazi homes.

Ein Volk, ein Reich, ein Führer.

the cultists proclaimed their Germanic purity and rededicated themselves to the "Germanic virtues" and to the eradication of Jewish influences in the Fatherland.

Also violently anti-Semitic was the Order of New Templars, founded in Austria around the turn of the century by a former Cistercian novice named Adolf Lanz. The New Templars were extremely selective: initiates had to pass muster as to their physical characteristics—some of the desirable features being blond hair, blue or gray eyes, a narrow, high-bridged nose, and slim hands and feet. In their Temples, located in several places throughout Austria, Germany, and Hungary, the members held "Grail celebrations," in which they practiced elaborate rituals.

Lanz met Hitler once, when the young house-painter came to his office in Vienna to pick up some back issues of the Templars' magazine. Some years later, just before the Nazis came to power, Lanz wrote to a fellow New Templar: "Hitler is one of our pupils

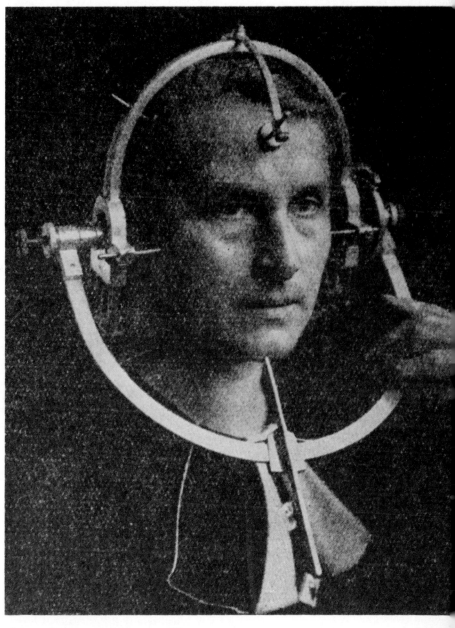

Above: back page of *Ostara*, a
magazine run by Adolf Lanz,
founder of the New Templars.
Lanz's quasi-religious Order had
strongly racist beliefs, and
selected its candidates carefully to ensure all its members
were of pure Germanic descent.
Its ultimate goal was the produc-
tion of a white master race but
because the movement never held
political power it was unable
to put its aims into effect.
Right: using a "platometer" to
measure whether the head of a
prospective member of the Germanen
Order conforms to "Nordic ideals."
Like the New Templars, the Germanen Order believed in a master
race, which was also to be purely
Germanic. The Order was anti-
Semitic and originated many ideas
in which the Nazis later believed.

. . . you will one day experience that he, and through him we, will
one day be victorious and develop a movement that makes the
world tremble."

But if Lanz acknowledged Hitler as one of his own, the Führer
did not return the compliment. Hitler regarded the New Templars
and the Völkisch cults with contempt, because they were politic-
ally ineffective. They talked, published, and performed rituals,
but never accomplished their goal of a racially "pure" society.
That could be accomplished only through the ruthless exercise of
power, as he proceeded to demonstrate.

Yet although none of these cults had many members (today
they are apparently extinct), they probably made some contribution to the success of the Nazi movement. By publicizing
and glamorizing their racist ideas they must have helped to make
anti-Semitism seem patriotic.

Of all racist cults the most powerful was undoubtedly the Ku

Above: Negro Federal troops
scatter before a Ku Klux Klansmen's charge, a scene from D. W.
Griffith's film *Birth of a
Nation*, made in 1915. The Klan
was originally founded after the
end of the Civil War to protect
white Southerners from the abuse
of the liberated Negro slaves,
but it persisted as a violently
racist cult even after its original purpose had disappeared.
Below: frontispiece of Thomas
Dixon's novel *The Clansman*, published in 1905, on which Griffith
based part of the plot of *Birth
of a Nation*. Dixon's book glorified the Ku Klux Klan as the
savior of the Southern whites.

Klux Klan. Born of the Southern whites' fear of retaliation from
freed slaves and originally intended as a sort of vigilante group,
the Klan of Reconstruction days quickly degenerated into gangs
of terrorists.

In time, Federal action against the Klan, combined with the
regaining of political control by whites in the South, caused the
Klan to disappear—temporarily. Then, around the beginning of
the 20th century, it reappeared. Shortly after the release of D. W.
Griffith's film *Birth of a Nation*, in which Klansmen were portrayed as heroes, a man named William Joseph Simmons
decided to take advantage of the newly stirring racism he detected
in the South. With 15 followers he climbed to the top of Stone
Mountain, near Atlanta, and there, beside a stone altar on which
lay the American flag, an open Bible, a sword, and a canteen of
holy water, he burned a cross and declared himself Grand Wizard.

The new Klan did not really get started until after World
War I, but then it spread through the United States with terrifying speed and force. By 1924 it had 4,000,000 members. Indiana
alone had 500,000 members, many of them filling political offices
throughout the state.

To the original anti-black obsession, the new Klansmen added
anti-Semitism and anti-Catholicism. They were rabid pro-
hibitionists and savage guardians of public morality. They saw
themselves as crusaders fighting against corruption. Appealing
simultaneously to racial, national, and religious prejudice, to
Grundyism, to a fascination with secret ceremonies in outlandish
costumes, and to the lust for power, the Klan was one of the most
successful and sinister bandwagons ever set in motion.

The Klan collapsed for a second time in the late 1920s. Its
decline was precipitated by the arrest and conviction of the
Indiana Grand Dragon, David C. Stephenson, for the rape,
mutilation, and murder of a young woman. This somewhat
tarnished the Klan's image as an upholder of morality, even
among the members themselves. People who had joined it
because it was the "thing to do" or "good for business" quickly

dropped out. A fierce Klan campaign against Al Smith in 1928 exhausted its funds. Only a hard core of fanatics now remained. The occasional lynching still occurred in the backwoods of the South, but the Klan was no longer a political force to be reckoned with. The FBI waged a vigorous campaign against it and largely succeeded in crippling it.

With the Supreme Court desegregation decision in 1954, the Klan rose again. It was responsible for much of the violence with which the South resisted integration, although many dedicated segregationists preferred to fight the Civil Rights Movement with the more sophisticated methods of the Citizens' Councils. The ludicrous trappings of the Klan have little appeal today. Its present membership is estimated at between 40,000 and 65,000 and is mainly confined to rural areas of the deep South, although branches exist in a few Northern states. It is generally regarded with contempt even among white segregationists. The evidence suggests that the Klan is going down for the third, and last, time.

Above: Robert Shelton, Imperial Wizard of the United Klans of America, at a rally in South Carolina in 1964. He wears the traditional costume of the Klansman and stands before a burning cross, symbol of the cult. The Klan has never hesitated to use violence in pursuit of its aims and it is suspected that the 27 civil rights supporters murdered in the South in 1960–65 were victims of the Klan. In 1965, President Johnson called for new legislation to suppress the Klan, but it still persists in rural areas of the South, though with greatly reduced power.

4

Love Sacred and Profane

Around the time of the Emperor Hadrian, when the early Christians were defining their beliefs, a man named Carpocrates, who lived in Egypt, offered a popular variation of the new religion. For one thing, he taught that Jesus had been born naturally of Joseph and Mary, and not by the Virgin Birth. He also maintained that people had a moral obligation to sin, for salvation logically implied a state of sin from which a person was saved. Lust, in his view, had been planted by God in the human soul precisely for this purpose, and therefore lust and its gratification were virtually obligatory. Moreover, he believed that God meant all possessions to be held in

Right: 19th-century French caricature of Barthélemy Prosper Enfantin with one of his female disciples. Enfantin's socialist sect believed in a God who combined male and female in one being and who should be served by a high priest—Le Père—and a high priestess—La Mère—merged in mystical and physical union. Enfantin, who was himself Le Père, spent much of his life searching for his female soulmate, La Mère.

"Sex outside marriage has usually been condemned as a sin"

common, and of course these "possessions" included women.

Among the many cults that flourished in the Roman Empire, Carpocrates' was—not surprisingly—one of the most attractive. For many people, no doubt, the Good News of Christianity was rendered even sweeter by this sanctioning of their natural inclinations. Plenty of people in ancient Rome (and before and since) could take their pleasure for its own sake, without trying to reconcile it with a moral code; but a great many other people have found that they feel better about sexual indulgence if they can find some justification for it. Carpocrates' cult was neither the first nor the last to offer such justification.

The early Church, as we know, repudiated such ideas, and its teachings about sex were strongly influenced by the writings of St. Paul, whose attitude toward the subject was one of grudging tolerance. "It is good for a man not to touch a woman," he wrote. "Nevertheless, to avoid fornication, let every man have his own wife . . .for it is better to marry than to burn."

Although the various branches of Christianity have taken a more positive view of marriage and conjugal love, there have always been some Christians who regard sexuality as an unfortunate aspect of humanity and who uphold celibacy as the better life. Moreover, sex outside marriage has usually been condemned as a sin, and those found guilty of it subjected to severe censure. Perhaps because lust and its gratification is arguably the most enjoyable of the Seven Deadly Sins, it has attracted more attention than the others. Christian society has never become so exercised about gluttony, envy, or pride, for example, as it has about lust. Among some people, in fact, the word "sin" is virtually synonymous with "sex."

This anti-sex attitude has never been more prevalent than it was in Britain and America during the 19th century. Extreme prudery (to the point of clothing piano legs) and a conviction that no "lady" could possibly enjoy sex were among the hallmarks of the age. Although many people did indulge their sexual appetites, most of them felt extremely guilty about it, and went to great lengths to conceal their transgression and preserve the mask of propriety.

It is not surprising that this period produced a variety of cults and religious sects whose distinguishing characteristic was their attitude toward sex. Some of them, following St. Paul, practiced celibacy. Some of them, reacting against the strict monogamy of Western society (and in particular the idea of a wife being her husband's property), practiced free love. A few catered to the hypocrisy of the age by disguising the gratification of natural desires as an expression of spirituality.

Foremost among the latter were the Agapemonites. Pronounced "a ga *pem* o nites," the name is derived from the Greek word *agapē*, meaning love of a spiritual kind—as opposed to *eros*, the Greek word for physical love. The name was also intended to suggest the love feasts, or *agapae*, of the early Christians. This sect was founded in England in the 1840s by the Rev. Henry James Prince. Prince had started his career in the Church of England, and he soon made a name for himself as an eloquent preacher. From miles around, people flocked to the little parish of Charlinch, in Somerset; and the ladies, in par-

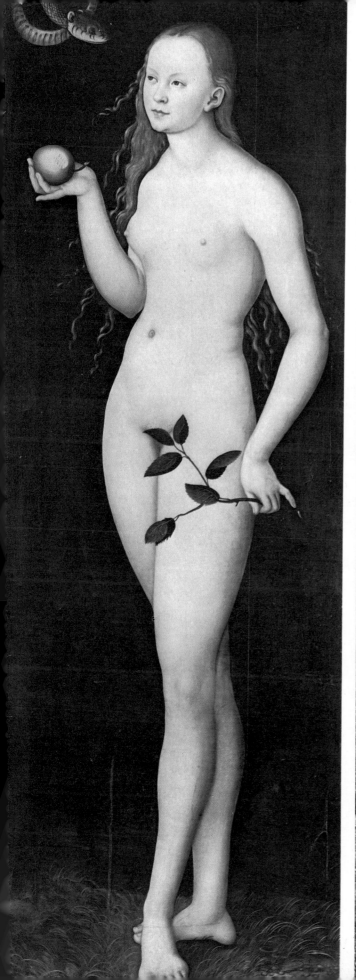

Left: Lucas Cranach's painting of Eve the temptress. Her appealing face and beautiful body symbolize the early Christian belief that woman is the stumbling block over which man falls into sin. In this view, sexual desire and its gratification—even within marriage—are sinful, and should not be condoned.
Below: *Early Lovers* by Frederick Smallfield. Prudery and revulsion against sex reached their height in the 19th century and, in keeping with conventions of the time, while these lovers' hands touch, their bodies are symbolically separated by a fence. In a society where natural desires were frowned upon, it is not surprising that cults which glorified physical relationships flourished.

Above: the Abode of Love, headquarters of the Agapemonites, in Spaxton, England. The Abode was bought by Henry Prince, founder of the sect, with money that was donated by his wealthy followers.
Right: John Smyth-Pigott, Henry Prince's successor as leader of the Agapemonites. Like Prince, John Smyth-Pigott was an ordained clergyman of the Church of England, but following their involvement with the Agapemonites, both men were dismissed by the Church.
Below: the Agapemonites' chapel. No expense was spared in its décor: the floor was of inlaid wood, and the pews were spangled with gold.

ticular, found Prince enthralling. Soon he made another kind of name for himself: rumors of scandalous behavior reached the ears of his bishop, and Prince was forbidden to preach within the church.

Undaunted, Prince and a fellow clergyman began preaching in the open, again with great popular success. He obtained his own chapel in fashionable Brighton and began attracting society people. He told his flock that he had been chosen by God to be the perfect man, incapable of sin. He was immortal, he claimed, and those who followed him would be immortal also. Furthermore, his followers could indulge in the sex act with no fear of sin. Prince once confided to a potential convert that the Song of Songs was for him "a divine revelation that life realized through the flesh was the ultimate expression of spirituality and love."

In spite of its official chastity Victorian England offered plenty of opportunities for gratifying the flesh—in London in 1868 there were some 18,000 prostitutes—but Prince would hardly have been satisfied with such furtive pleasures. Sex garbed in sanctity was what he required, and he set about arranging it.

Having extracted large sums of money from his wealthy followers—the price of immortality being the bulk of one's fortune—Prince acquired a 200-acre estate near Spaxton, in Somerset, and named it the Agapemone, or Abode of Love. The existing buildings—a large house, stables, cottages, and an unfinished church—he refurbished at considerable expense, to accommodate in luxury the 60 disciples who joined him in the Abode. They were housed according to the amount of money they contributed to the establishment. Besides the "Beloved One," as Prince now styled himself, only women disciples lived in the main house.

The main room of the house was the chapel, an extraordinary room fitted not only with the customary altar, organ, and stained glass windows, but also with a billiard table. Here the faithful could enjoy a game or relax with a glass of sherry from the well-stocked cellars. Here, they held occasional religious services, although these became more infrequent as the years passed. Here, too, they witnessed the Great Manifestation.

In this ceremony Prince surpassed himself in hypocrisy and blasphemy. He had already seduced a number of his female disciples, virtually under the eyes of his middle-aged wife, but he became obsessed with the idea of taking a young and beautiful virgin as his special mistress. The girl he selected was an orphan named Zoë Paterson, who had been brought to the Abode by her widowed mother. The mother had died, leaving Zoë, then in her teens and remarkably beautiful, in the care of the Beloved One. Prince cunningly paved the way for his appropriation of Zoë by announcing to his flock that God had appointed him to purge the community of all sin and that the means of so doing was for him to take a young virgin as his "Bride of the Lamb." Who this bride was to be Prince claimed not to know, but he assured them that God would reveal her identity in His good time.

Accordingly one evening the faithful gathered in the chapel, and in an atmosphere of incense, candlelight, and soft music from the organ, witnessed the choosing of the Bride of the Lamb. Heralded by trumpets and wearing silken robes, Prince strode

Bride of the Lamb

Among the most blatantly sexual of the sects that sprang up in response to the prudery of Victorian England was the Agapemonites, whose name was derived from the Greek word *agapē*, meaning "spiritual love." But despite the sect's name, the desires of its founder, Henry Prince, were material rather than spiritual. Prince desired first wealth, then sex.

His more normal lusts sated, Prince, who called himself the "Beloved One," became obsessed with the idea of seducing a young virgin, Zoë Paterson. To make her seduction respectable, at least in the eyes of his disciples, Prince had to cover his plot by an elaborate farce. Telling the Agapemonites that God had chosen him to cleanse the community of sin by taking a young virgin as his "Bride of the Lamb," Prince commanded all his followers to gather in the chapel where, he said, God would make known his choice of a bride.

When Prince entered the chapel, he walked straight to Zoë Paterson, declaring that she was the Bride of the Lamb. But once their "spiritual" union was physically sealed, part of Prince's fraud was exposed. For although he had declared that the faithful need undergo neither childbirth nor death, in due course Zoë presented him with a son.

Right: Sister Ruth's coffin lies in the chapel in Spaxton. "Sister Ruth" was the name given by the Agapemonites to Ruth Anne Preece, whom Smyth-Pigott took as his "Chief Soul Bride" in 1904. Despite this mystical title, Sister Ruth's relationship with Smyth-Pigott was that of an earthly wife to her husband, and she bore him three children.
Below: Ruth Anne Preece, "Sister Ruth." When in time Smyth-Pigott tired of his Chief Soul Bride and attempted to replace her, Sister Ruth was wildly jealous. She was publicly repudiated by Smyth-Pigott, and stripped of her emblems of rank and official robes, and soon afterward she left the Abode of Love for a time.

through the disciples, then came to a halt before the frightened 16-year-old Zoë. He kissed her, pronounced her the chosen one, and led her by the hand to his private apartments.

In time, Zoë produced a child. This was not the first child fathered by the Beloved One at the Abode; other offspring had been delivered in Bristol, then brought back to Spaxton. When visitors called, the children were kept out of sight, for in theory childbirth, like death, would be waived for the Beloved's followers. Zoë's pregnancy was particularly embarrassing, for as the "Bride of the Lamb," she was presumably united to Prince only in a mystical relationship. After announcing defiantly that there would be no birth, Prince explained the undeniable arrival of his son as "Satan's final despairing act against God."

After this event, some of the flock began to have doubts about the Beloved and his claims, and some of them left. Occasionally, lawsuits were brought against Prince by relatives of the women he had lured to the Abode and divested of their fortunes. He was forced to repay thousands of pounds, and to make certain economies at the Abode. Those disciples who had no money left to contribute were drafted into domestic service. Prince remained dictator of the establishment. He was even able to persuade his followers—including married couples—to abstain from sexual intercourse; only he, the Beloved One, was chosen to partake of this pleasure. Sloth, not lust, was the prevailing sin at the Agapemone in the declining years of the Prince regime. The members ate and drank, dozed, and played billiards.

When, in 1899, Prince appalled his followers by dying like any other human being, it looked as though the Abode might shut its doors. One enterprising disciple, however, set out to find a new Messiah. He found one in the person of the Rev. John Hugh Smyth-Pigott, another Church of England clergyman with a gift for oratory and a way with women. Smyth-Pigott proclaimed himself the new Messiah from the pulpit of a splendid church in London that the Agapemonites had built in their days of prosperity but that had failed to attract a congregation—largely,

Above: mourners entering the grounds of the Abode of Love to attend Smyth-Pigott's funeral. One of the principal tenets of the creed preached by Prince and Smyth-Pigott was that they were immortal, and that neither they nor those who believed in them would ever die. But to their followers' consternation, in time both men did die.
Right: Smyth-Pigott shortly before his death in 1927 at the age of 75.

no doubt, because the sect's leaders were too attached to the *dolce far niente* at Spaxton. After a very brief ministry at the London church—marred occasionally by hostile mobs—Smyth-Pigott, too, retreated to the Abode of Love.

There, he followed in the footsteps of his predecessor, taking a succession of "soul brides," as he called them, from among the 50 or so pretty, educated young women who constituted his Upper Circle of disciples. His wife Catherine seems to have been the only resident of the Agapemone to have practiced *agapē*; she won the affection of the village for her visits to the sick and the elderly, and gifts of food to the poor. Smyth-Pigott ignored her. After two years' residence in Spaxton, he took a "Chief Soul Bride," a beautiful girl with very soulful eyes, named Ruth

71

Above: John Noyes, founder of the Oneida Community. Noyes' followers were at first known as Perfectionists, because Noyes believed that man could become perfect, completely free from the possibility of sin. They became known as the Oneida Community after establishing themselves in Oneida, New York. There, the sect ran a community that was communist in bias, with children as well as property considered as belonging to the group, rather than to its individual members.

Above right: members of the Oneida Community play a game of croquet on their estate. The community abolished marriage but, contrary to popular belief, did not practice free love: pairings were arranged by Noyes with a view to producing the best children possible. American society was scandalized by what it considered moral laxity, and it was with a view to disproving such beliefs that women members wore this form of dress, designed principally with modesty in view.

Right: an early-20th-century photograph of a factory belonging to the Oneida Community. The community engaged successfully in various commercial pursuits, and although as a sect it has long vanished, as a manufacturing company it survives to this day.

Anne Preece. "Sister" Ruth bore Smyth-Pigott three children.

In time, inevitably, Smyth-Pigott began to favor a younger recruit, and when Ruth vented her jealousy in an angry outburst, he punished her by publicly repudiating her in the chapel and installing the current favorite, Sister Grace, as the new Chief Soul Bride. Ruth was ceremonially stripped of her emblems of rank and even of her robes. She bore her humiliation stoically, but shortly afterward she left the Abode, which had been her home for 15 years. Deprived of her children by the command of the Beloved One, she wandered around England at loose ends until finally, after receiving overtures from Smyth-Pigott, she consented to return. But it was the community, not the Beloved One, that she missed; Smyth-Pigott had lost his power over her, and she now felt only pity for him.

In 1927, at the age of 75, Smyth-Pigott, like Prince before him, embarrassed his followers by dying. He was buried in the grounds of the Agapemone, and his funeral was attended by followers from other parts of England and even from Norway and France, where he had established several outposts of the faith. For another 30 years, the Abode continued in operation. Its numbers dwindled, and it became a kind of secluded guest house. A young girl who was taken there by her strict maiden aunt shortly after Smyth-Pigott's death was disappointed to find that there was none of the flirtation and dressing up that she had innocently expected. "No man ever made a pass at me the whole time, nor at any of the other girls as far as I know. . . . Life at the Abode was really very depressing."

Even in their heyday, the Agapemonites hardly qualified as a free-love community. Their sexual beliefs and practices were so enmeshed with the personality cult of the two Beloved Ones— who seem to have had a monopoly of the activity—and so overlaid with pretense that it is hard to determine what they actually believed.

By contrast, their contemporaries the Perfectionists had a more democratic conception of love between the sexes. This American sect was founded by John Humphrey Noyes in the 1840s, when religious enthusiasm was sweeping the United States and when experiments in communal living were also flourishing. Noyes taught that after being converted to Christianity, people might receive a second blessing and that after this sanctification they would be unable to sin: that is, they could behave promiscuously without fear of having sinned. He also believed that when God's will was truly done on earth there would be no sexual relations; but that before this state arrived it was necessary to abolish marriage, with the possessiveness it entailed. Property, too, would be held in common. After a brief stay in Putney, Vermont, where they met with public hostility, the Perfectionists moved to Oneida, New York, where they became known as the Oneida Community.

Outsiders were intrigued and scandalized by the Oneida Community's unconventional life and by statements such as the following, from a pamphlet by Noyes:

"The new commandment is that we love one another, and that not in pairs but *en masse*. We are required to love one another fervently; the fashion of the world forbids a man and a woman

The Walworth Jumpers

Around 1870, under a converted railroad arch off southeast London's Walworth Road, a Suffolk woman called Mary Ann Girling began a mission to convert the people of London to her creed of celibacy, immortality, and communal life. Her followers called themselves Bible Christians, but they were generally known as the Walworth Jumpers because of the way they danced while in a religious trance. In 1873, the Jumpers founded a community in the New Forest.

The New Forest community was strictly controlled by Mrs. Girling, who devised a code of rules to keep her followers strong in the faith. The first set out the conditions of purity and holiness necessary for admission to the community, but the other seven governed the conduct of its members. All property, including gifts, had to be given up to Mrs. Girling for equal distribution; correspondence with family and friends was forbidden, and all letters censored; and without permission no one could leave the community grounds. No "undue intimacy" was permitted between sect members, and the bringing up of all children was left to Mrs. Girling alone. Had she been an efficient administrator, her colony might have prospered.

who are otherwise appropriated to love one another fervently, but if they obey Christ they must do this . . . love is not a sin. Susceptibility to love is not burnt out by one honeymoon or satisfied with one love. On the contrary, the more you do the more you can. It is the law of nature."

In fact, love in the Oneida Community was not quite so free as these words would suggest. In the interest of producing the best possible offspring, Noyes paired certain people together, temporarily. Exclusive affections were discouraged. Children were reared by the community; no child was considered to belong to his mother or father. It was a highly organized community with a strong moral code.

Moreover, it was an industrious and prosperous one. The Perfectionists owned 600 acres of forest land, farmed, ran a lumber mill, manufactured steel traps, and ran a cannery. Five years after its founding, the community's assets were valued at $67,000.

Eventually, however, so much pressure was brought to bear upon the community that they abandoned their system of "complex marriage." After 1880, the religious character of the group had virtually disappeared, and today the Oneida Community survives only in the form of the manufacturing company the members created.

At the same time that Noyes was establishing the Oneida Community, an English-born preacher named Thomas Lake Harris formed the Brotherhood of the New Life. For a while the Brotherhood lived in Mountain Cove, Virginia, which they believed was the site of the original Garden of Eden. Later, they settled by Lake Erie, in New York. They believed that God was both male and female, and they also believed that people had a duty to love each other physically and promiscuously. Harris, known as Father, ruled the sect along with his bride, called Lily Queen. Members of the Brotherhood surrendered to him their worldly possessions and worked the land for the common good.

The sect remained small, but it did attract one distinguished member, the English Member of Parliament Laurence Oliphant. He had been captivated by Harris's mystical authority—reminiscent of that of an Old Testament prophet—when Harris visited London in 1864. He agreed to join Harris in the United States.

Having turned his money over to Harris, Oliphant spent two years on probation with the Brotherhood, working, eating, and sleeping alone, forbidden by Harris even to talk to the others. His mother joined him there and worked as cook and kitchen maid. After two years, Harris sent Oliphant back to England, where he worked as a war correspondent for *The Times* and lived on a small allowance provided by Harris, while sending his earnings to the Brotherhood. When he decided to get married, he wrote to Harris for permission, and his wife sent all her money to the Brotherhood. On Harris's command, the Oliphants went to the United States; but they had no sooner arrived than Harris separated them. He sent Oliphant back to London to earn more money, and took Mrs. Oliphant and most of the Brotherhood to their new settlement in California.

Eventually, Oliphant (back in the United States) regained his senses sufficiently to sue Harris for his money, whereupon Harris tried to have him declared insane. Oliphant and his wife fled the country.

They settled in Haifa, in Palestine, where they set up their own cult devoted to what they called *Sympneumata*, or the union of spiritual and earthly counterparts. They believed that it was only through maintaining a state of sexual excitement that one could become spiritually alive. To promote this state, they advocated the practice of lying together but abstaining from intercourse. A writer describing the cult noted that Mrs. Oliphant would often get into bed with men who were extremely dirty: "The contact of her body brought about, as she supposed, the coming of the [spiritual] counterpart. It was a great trial to her to do this, and she felt that she was performing a most holy mission." The Oliphants' cult disintegrated after the founders died, toward the end of the century.

Whereas some people sought spiritual enlightenment through sex—or found spiritual disguises for sexual motives—other groups practiced celibacy.

One of these was the Walworth Jumpers, founded in Suffolk, England, around 1870 by Mary Ann Girling. Married to a sailor, Mrs. Girling spent most of her first 12 years of marriage in pregnancy. She had 10 children, two of whom died. Her husband was, of course, away much of the time; and at one point, overcome with melancholy, she turned to religion.

Soon she began having visions of Christ, who told her that his second coming was imminent and that she was to bring this news to the world. After beginning his mission in Suffolk, Mary Ann Girling went on to London, where she preached under a railroad arch near Walworth Road. As in many other revivalist sects, her followers went into religious ecstasies, leaping about in a state of semitrance. Popularly called the Walworth Jumpers, they preferred the name Bible Christians. They regarded celibacy as the secret of eternal life—reasoning that death was the penalty for sin, and therefore, to be celibate was to be sinless and so to live forever. Implicit in this reasoning was the exclusive identification of sin with sex, characteristic of the age.

Mother Girling and her 160 followers eventually settled on a small estate in the New Forest. A code of rules imposed by Mother Girling included the censorship of letters, the communal ownership of property, and, of course, celibacy. Unfortunately Mrs. Girling was a poor administrator, and the community soon suffered economic hardship. Cold, hunger, and the resultant illness claimed a number of the faithful. Their deaths were explained by Mother Girling as the result of sin.

As the sect's numbers dwindled, their leader became more fanatical. She claimed to be "both Mother and Savior." She was not merely the messenger of Christ's second coming; she *was* the second coming. Her flock, mostly women, sang hymns to her and danced around her. In 1885 she became ill, and her illness was diagnosed as cancer. For nearly a year she suffered great pain, still insisting she would never die. With her death, the cult finally disintegrated, 16 years after its founding.

The Walworth Jumpers were sometimes compared to the Shakers, another celibate group, led by a woman, who worshiped

Above: Laurence Oliphant, British Member of Parliament and later war correspondent of *The Times*, was also founder of *Sympneumata*, one of the world's strangest sex cults. Sympneumata involved maintaining a state of intense sexual excitement through bodily contact, but without actually having intercourse: the act was considered particularly blessed if one of the parties was thoroughly undesirable. Earlier, Oliphant had joined Thomas Harris's Brotherhood of the New Life in America, and it may have been from the Brotherhood's beliefs in physical and promiscuous love that Oliphant's sexual missionary fervor sprang.

Left: Mother Ann Lee, founder of the Shakers. The official title of the movement is the United Society of Believers in Christ's Second Coming, and the Shakers believe that Christ has returned for a second time—but in female form, as Ann Lee. Shaker doctrine is based on the belief that the original sin in the Garden of Eden was sexual intercourse, and sex is strictly forbidden to members of the sect, who must foreswear marriage when they join.

through dancing. Founded in England in the mid-1700s by a young woman named Ann Lee, the Shakers—or United Society of Believers in Christ's Second Coming—soon emigrated to the United States. By the early 1800s they had established 20 communities, and the sect continued to flourish until the beginning of this century, when it began to decline. Today, only a few of its disciples are still alive.

Mother Lee had been married, but one day, she claimed, God revealed to her that the original sin in the Garden of Eden—and the cause of all evil in the world—was sexual intercourse. She separated from her husband, who found her preaching so convincing that he became one of her disciples. Other married couples sometimes joined the Shakers, forsaking the "marriage

Above: Shakers dancing at a religious service. The Shaker life is a communal one, sober, frugal, and hard-working, and the only outlet for emotion is the dance that characterizes Shaker worship, and from which the sect derives its name. While Shakers dance, they tremble from the intensity of their religious ecstasy. Left: a woman Shaker heads for the "sisters' door" in a Shaker meeting house in Maine in 1974. The Shakers used to adopt children to bring up in the faith, but the custom is dying out and the sect has few followers today.

SHAKER
MEETING HOUSE
1794

of the flesh" and living in celibacy. In a Shaker colony both sexes lived in the same house, but slept in dormitories at opposite ends of the building. Their life was characterized by hard work, frugality, and sobriety. They dressed like Quakers. In their worship, however, they let themselves go a little. Besides the usual hymns and anthems, the service included marching and communal dancing. Men and women danced in their respective groups, and occasionally a single dancer would whirl about like a dervish.

Central to the Shaker creed was the belief that God was both male and female. The first coming of Christ, in the form of Jesus, had been followed, they believed, by the second coming as a woman: Mother Ann Lee. One member of the sect wrote this description of the Shaker concept of heaven:

"Heaven is a Shaker community on a very large scale. Everything is spiritual. Jesus Christ is the Head Elder, and Mother

Above: Barthélemy Enfantin in later life. The enthusiasm that enabled Enfantin to promote his own semireligious socialist sect in the face of general ridicule later brought him business success. In the early days of the railroad, he believed strongly enough in its future to become chief promoter of the Paris-Lyons-Méditerranée line. After 1856, as its General Manager and in cooperation with its labor force, he was able to try out many of his socialist ideals.

Ann is the Head Eldress. The buildings are large and splendid, being all of white marble. There are large orchards with all kinds of fruit . . . but all is spiritual. Outside of this heaven the spirits of the departed wander about on the surface of the earth—which is the Shaker hell—till they are converted to Shakerism."

Although their vision of the Millennium was never realized, the Shakers must at least be credited with having practiced what they preached. For more than 100 years they maintained a communistic utopia based on Christian principles. Outsiders marveled at the harmony in which they lived together. Their way of life was too spartan and ascetic to gain it many converts in the modern world—and of course it depended absolutely on converts, as there were no offspring—but by successfully practicing brotherly love the Shakers were a beacon of hope to other utopians.

A quite different utopian society, based partly on physical love, was proposed by a Frenchman. Barthélemy Prosper Enfantin started his career, around the time of Napoleon, as a bank employee. Soon he became converted to the theories of Saint-Simon, founder of French socialism. Building on Saint-Simon's ideas of equality and a reorganization of the economic structure, Enfantin advocated a society in which women would be treated as equals and freed from their vows of obedience and fidelity to men, and in which temporary marriages would be considered as legitimate as permanent ones. He taught that matter as well as spirit is divine. Like Mother Lee, he believed that God is both male and female, but he arrived at a different conclusion from this premise: the couple, in which self merged with non-self, was sacred. And Enfantin himself, who had messianic notions and called himself "le Père," must find "la Mère." Their mating, he said, would produce a new revelation.

La Mère was sought in far-flung countries, from Turkey to America, but none of the candidates measured up to expectations. (The woman novelist George Sand was approached but she declined the honor.) Around 1830, Enfantin settled down in a suburb of Paris called Menilmontant with 40 disciples—all

Left: the house in Menilmontant owned by Enfantin's mother. Enfantin inherited this house on the outskirts of Paris when his mother died in 1832, and he immediately established himself there with 40 of his disciples to await the arrival of his high priestess, La Mère.

male. There, he awaited the arrival of the promised Mother. Somewhat inconsistently, in view of his liberal speeches about women and the holiness of the flesh, he commanded his followers to be celibate. Some returned to their wives, but others obediently declared their marriages void.

In Menilmontant Enfantin's followers, dressed in picturesque uniforms of red, white, and blue, led a strictly organized life, getting up at 5:00 a.m., doing the housework, and pursuing courses of study, including geography, geology, and music. Le Père busied himself with plans for the New City that he would someday establish.

Before his plans for the city got off the drawing board, the government—fearing the influence of his revolutionary ideas—

Right: caricature of Enfantin's followers entitled *The Monks of Menilmontant, or the abilities of the Saint-Simoniens!* Despite Enfantin's belief in the liberty of the sexes and free marriage, the Menilmontant community was composed entirely of men, all of whom had taken vows of chastity. Enfantin and his followers believed that a paid domestic was just a slave and carried out all the household duties themselves, to the amusement of French society and the Parisian cartoonists.

Right: Henri de Saint-Simon, social reformer and the founder of French socialism. Saint-Simon propounded a utopian society in which the inheritance of wealth would be abolished, women emancipated, and working men set free from their bonds. Enfantin's doctrine was based on that of Saint-Simon, but to Saint-Simon's beliefs Enfantin added a mystical element. He believed in a God combining male and female, and in the consequent need for his prophet Le Père to find La Mère.

tried Enfantin for "outrage against public morality" and threw
him in jail for one year. After that, Enfantin never mustered
much popular enthusiasm for his cause. After trying his hand at
a number of trades and professions, he ended up as General
Manager of the Paris-Lyons-Méditerranée railroad.

But one of his female disciples, Léonore Labillière, had been
fired with the idea of establishing a community that really would
practice free love. In the 1830s and 1840s she toured Europe and
the United States, investigating the experiments then under way.
She visited the Oneida Community, and in England she met
H. J. Prince, who was about to set up his Agapemone. Although
she found him fascinating and often went to hear him preach,
she also recognized him for "a hypocrite, a charlatan, and an un-
democratic spirit." Prince's efforts to get Léonore into his
Abode were unsuccessful.

Her travels convinced Léonore that most love cults had the
wrong approach. The religious element and the dictatorial
structure of the cults she visited interfered, in her opinion, with
the development of truly free love: "I have learned that you
cannot expect love to flourish or to prosper in a religious
atmosphere where love means whatever suits the whims of the
leader at any given moment. Abstinence and chastity one day,
when it suits him to proclaim their alleged virtues, sheer unrestrained lechery the next—the more unrestrained because of
the bogus abstinence which has gone before it. . . . Freedom in
love means . . . the freedom to love whom one pleases without
placing ridiculous obstacles in the way. But free love ought not
to mean promiscuity, but merely a license to find one's true
partner by a process of experiment."

Accordingly, she established her own abode of love, called
La Maison des Poètes (the House of Poets), in a rather run-down
house high in the Pyrenees. The romantic setting suited the

romantic ideals that underlay the experiment. Léonore wanted to revive the spirit of courtly love as practiced by the troubadours of medieval France. Her idea was that a man would court his love through verse and song in what she termed "an apprenticeship of spiritual love," and the woman was free to respond physically or not as she chose.

The women Léonore brought with her to the Maison des Poètes included several widows and women who had been disillusioned with love in conventional society. The men were unsuccessful artists in need of a handout. They worked for their keep, and they shared in the housework (perhaps the most revolutionary of all her ideas). Evenings were devoted to elegance: candlelit dinners, serenades, sparkling conversation led by Léonore.

Inevitably, the reality did not measure up to the ideal. Although her "poètes" gave lip service to the troubadour ideal, most of them merely wanted some creature comforts with no commitment. A few managed a quick seduction and then escaped into the less idealistic world outside. Some of the women took advantage of the "spiritual apprentice" idea to indulge in a bit of torture.

"Lucille has kept poor Pedro in a state of agony for weeks," wrote Léonore, "now encouraging him, then persuading him she requires more proof of his chivalry before she will allow him to become a supplicant. As for Rodrigue, poor man, he has been here a year and is still only allowed the merest morsels of love— to be permitted to undress Renée and then be told to leave her room. Once he was permitted to remain in her room all night, but merely to attend to her little wants, never to make love."

Léonore herself was already middle-aged, and her own attempts to find a devoted lover among the small, transient population of the Maison des Poètes were not rewarded. A few years after its founding, she fell ill and was forced to abandon the experiment.

Today, the more relaxed morals of society in general have lessened the need for love cults. One can practice free love without cloaking it in religious or political theory. The rich young ladies who ran away to Spaxton to join Prince and Smyth-Pigott because they thought it offered a spiritual alternative to conventional marriage would today have little trouble finding more attractive and more honest alternatives.

Even so, the idealists are always with us, trying to find new and more satisfactory ways to arrange things between the sexes. The love cult of the late 20th century is the hippie commune. After the complicated theories and the messianic delusions of earlier love cults, the simplicity of the hippie way of love seems rather refreshing. Their dedication to *eros* and *agapē* seems to combine the best elements of the 19th-century cults: brotherly love without the unnatural restraints of celibacy; sensual love without exploitation. Even those people who could not endure communal living themselves may admire the idealism and the gentleness of the hippie experiments. But love is a more complex emotion than many hippies suppose, and many a commune has broken up when the *eros* got a bit uncontrolled and the *agapē* wore a bit thin. On the whole, the lesson that emerges from the history of love cults is that love is too mysterious to be organized.

Right: a hippie wedding near San Francisco in the late 1960s. The hippie commune is the 20th-century manifestation of the love cults of earlier times, an attempt to combine physical passion with a general love for, and caring about, mankind. But in the freer, more permissive atmosphere of the present day, the hippies can live out their beliefs publicly, with no need for the religious trappings necessary in centuries gone by.

5

The Messiahs

"Every man would like to be God, if it were possible," said the philosopher Bertrand Russell; "some few find it difficult to admit the impossibility." People who suffer from the delusion that they are the reincarnation of Christ, or God's deputy on earth, are to be found in the schizophrenic wards of many mental hospitals. There, they are treated with the usual methods considered appropriate to their illness.

Occasionally, however, someone comes along who not only thinks he is the Messiah but also manages to convince others that he is. A private delusion becomes a public delusion and a cult is born. Within the

Right: an early-19th-century satirical drawing lampooning the prophetess Joanna Southcott. On the basis of prophecies given to her, she believed, by supernatural voices, Joanna acquired a large following and her sect had chapels throughout Britain. In her mid-60s, to the joy of her many disciples and the ridicule of others, she announced that she would shortly give birth to a child, the Second Messiah promised in the Book of Revelation. Her pregnancy was confirmed by a number of doctors, but when she died soon afterward she was found to have been suffering from an enlargement of the womb. Many of Joanna Southcott's contemporaries claimed that the child she was supposedly carrying was not God's, as Joanna asserted, but that of the Devil, portrayed as Parson Towser in this cartoon.

85

"Messiahs have often appeared when people were frightened, oppressed..."

Christian world, the belief in the second coming of Christ has inadvertently paved the way for bogus messiahs. This was particularly true in past centuries and among ignorant people. Given an uneducated population ready to believe in a returned Christ, a persuasive, charismatic personality who proclaimed his divinity with real conviction would be sure to win followers.

A typical false messiah of medieval times was a man named Tanchelm, a clerk employed by a Flemish nobleman in the 12th century. He first attracted popular support with his denunciations of the wealth of the Church and the financial burden it placed upon the people. As he gained more followers, he began to enlarge his claims. He asserted that he was possessed of the Holy Spirit to the same degree as Jesus had been. His adherents went along with his claim to divinity—even to the point of drinking his bathwater, which they believed capable of curing illnesses. Tanchelm was killed by a priest in 1115, but his cult persisted for many years after his death.

Messiahs have often appeared when people were frightened, oppressed, and looking for someone to lead them out of their troubles. This was the situation in the early 1500s in Germany and the Low Countries, where an impoverished peasantry began to believe that bad harvests, rampant inflation, and outbreaks of plague signaled the approaching end of the world. Sporadic peasant uprisings were put down with a ferocity that only strengthened the resolve of many rebels to gain revenge.

The break with the Roman Catholic Church, initiated by Martin Luther in 1517, opened the door to other dissenting sects. Among them were the Anabaptists, whose name, meaning "to baptize again," referred to their doctrine that infant baptism was meaningless and that one must be baptized as an adult. The Anabaptists drew their support mainly from the poor, especially the peasants. Preaching that the established governments were about to be destroyed and that the poor would inherit the earth and its riches, as well as eternal life, the Anabaptists were obvious candidates for persecution. Both Lutheran and Catholic rulers did their best to stamp out the movement, but without success.

Driven from their homes in other German and Dutch towns, Anabaptists were attracted to the city of Münster by several sympathizers already living there. Nominally ruled by a Catholic prince-bishop, Münster had become, by the 1530s, a mainly Lutheran city. The Anabaptists began to pour in to Münster, under two Dutch leaders of the movement: Jan Matthijszoon and his right-hand man Jan Bockelszoon. Matthijszoon, a strikingly handsome man, made a dramatic appearance in the marketplace, accompanied by his beautiful ex-nun wife and the equally attractive Bockelszoon. Both men wore flowing robes suitable to prophets, and Matthijszoon carried two stone tablets. He told the amazed townspeople that "the Lord has ordained me to impart His will to you." Bockelszoon, he told them, would "instruct you in the pure and holy service of God as is proper to a Chosen People."

These imposing prophets quickly gained local support, particularly from the women, who reacted in somewhat the same way as modern-day fans of pop stars—except that their enthusiasm was ostensibly religious. A contemporary account of the

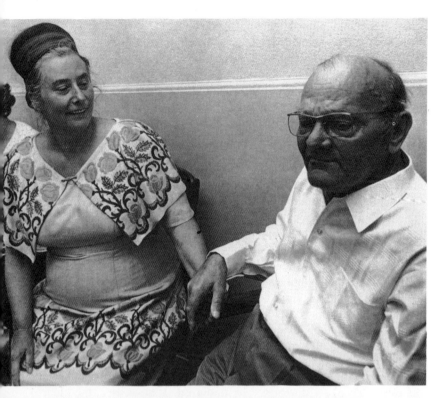

Left: the Second Coming, 20th-century style. In 1950, Louwrens van Voorthuizen, a Dutch fisherman, announced that he was God. He declared established religion and the Bible irrelevant now that God was again on earth and, in common with other messianic figures, prophesied the coming end of the world. Then, according to his doctrine, his followers alone would be saved. Despite his claim to immortality, he died in 1968, 18 years after founding his cult.

Below: a meeting of the followers of van Voorthuizen in 1967, the year before their leader's death. Van Voorthuizen preferred to be called Lou, and his disciples called themselves the *Loumensen*, or Lou's people. Although it continued as a group after Lou's death, without his inspiration the sect in time collapsed.

Below: Jan Matthijszoon, leader of the Anabaptists who took over the city of Münster in 1534. The Anabaptist sect, named for their belief that only adult baptism had value, drew their support from the poor who would, in their view, inherit the earth. To medieval rulers, this doctrine smacked of revolution and in many places Anabaptists were persecuted. Dutch and German members of the sect fled to Münster where there were sympathizers with their beliefs.

IOAN MATHYS VAN HAERLEM

events in Münster, written by a man hostile to the Anabaptists, gives a vivid—if perhaps exaggerated—picture of the hysteria: "The madness of the pagan bacchantes—cannot have surpassed that of these women. . . . Some had their hair disordered, others ran about almost naked . . . others again flung themselves on the ground with arms extended in the shape of a cross; then rose, clapped their hands, knelt down and cried, grinding their teeth, foaming at the mouth, beating their breasts, weeping, laughing, howling, and uttering the most strange, inarticulate sounds."

Within a month of the arrival of Matthijszoon and Bockelszoon, the Anabaptists had gained control of the Great Council of Münster. One of their first acts was to expel the city's remaining Lutherans and Catholics—except those willing to be converted. The refugees' possessions were confiscated, thrown into the common storehouse, and distributed among the Anabaptists.

Meanwhile, the prince-bishop of Münster and the governments of neighboring principalities assembled troops and encircled the city. Matthijszoon, too, organized an army. One day, acting on a vision he had had, Matthijszoon led 20 of his men outside the city walls to engage the enemy. The little band and their leader were quickly dispatched by the besiegers.

At that point, Bockelszoon took command. "God shall raise up unto us another prophet who shall be greater and higher than was even Jan Matthijszoon," he declared. It soon became clear who that was. Bockelszoon began by reorganizing the city's government. He was to be king of the "New Jerusalem," and 12 elders, symbolizing the 12 Tribes of Israel, would help him to administer the law.

There were plenty of new laws to administer: laws dealing with the communal ownership of property; laws permitting polygamy and divorce; laws stipulating the death penalty for various offenses including blasphemy and the refusal, by a woman, to marry any man who chose her. There was a great surplus of women in Münster, so the polygamy statute was doubtless viewed favorably by many, but the lack of choice was a drawback.

Bockelszoon himself eventually took 16 wives, his queen being Matthijszoon's beautiful widow Divara. He set up an elaborate court and dressed himself and his wives in silks and gold. (His subjects were required by law to dress plainly—most of their clothes were confiscated.) A goldsmith named Dusentscheuer fashioned gold crowns and elaborate pieces of jewelry for the king and queen. Dusentscheuer also served as Bockelszoon's "prophet," or public relations man. He would run through the streets crying, "Jan Bockelszoon of Leyden, the saint and prophet of God, must be king of the whole earth. His authority will extend over emperors, kings, and princes, and all the powers of the world, and none shall rise above him. He will occupy the throne of his father, David, and will carry the scepter till the Lord reclaims it from him." Commemorative medallions were struck depicting Bockelszoon's head, surrounded by the inscription: "The Word Was Made Flesh."

To his credit, Bockelszoon did manage to defend the city effectively for well over a year. Short of manpower, he drafted the women, who learned to use the crossbow and to prepare the lime and boiling pitch used against attacking forces. Inevitably,

however, the blockade around the city had its effect. The Münsterites gradually starved, while Bockelszoon promised them miracles. God would turn the cobblestones into bread, he told them. The despairing Münsterites turned to promiscuous sex as their one temporary escape from suffering. The last days of Bockelszoon's reign were a protracted, joyless orgy.

Finally, Bockelszoon allowed those who wished to leave the city to do so, telling them they would pay for their cowardice with everlasting damnation. The fugitives certainly paid a physical price: the able-bodied men were promptly killed by the enemy; the old men, women, and children were not allowed to pass through the encircling troops but were confined to the no man's land between the city and the army. They crawled around eating grass, while their coreligionists jeered at them from the battlements. One night one of these exiles showed the soldiers a secret way into the city. The enemy crept in, and after a day of savage fighting, the Anabaptists were finally vanquished.

Bockelszoon and a few of his deputies were arrested and then taken on a tour of some of the German towns, where they were exhibited on chains like captured wild beasts. Then they were brought back to Münster and in the main square were tortured to death. Bockelszoon's mutilated body was put in an iron cage and hung from the church of St. Lambert.

The defeat of the Münster Anabaptists put an end to the sect's militant aspirations, but many of its peaceful adherents thought it best to move to England. Throughout the 16th century and most of the 17th, that country saw a profusion of new sects, often led by self-proclaimed messiahs. Intermittent persecution caused many of these groups to emigrate to America, but new ones were forever springing up.

Right: Jan Bockelszoon, leader with Matthijszoon of the Münster Anabaptists. The two men succeeded in increasing local support for the Anabaptists, and within a month of their arrival in the city had gained control of the council. Local princes, afraid of possible repercussions, sent forces to overthrow the Anabaptist rulers, and in the skirmish with these forces Matthijszoon was killed. Bockelszoon then declared himself the divinely appointed King of Münster. During his short reign he lived in considerable splendor, in contrast with Anabaptist ideals. Below: Divara, once a nun, had later become the wife of Jan Matthijszoon. After his death, she married Jan Bockelszoon and when he declared himself King of Münster, Divara became his queen.

IOHAN·VÁ·LEIDEN·EY·KONINCK·DER·WEDERDOPER·
THO·MONSTER·WA   ERHAFTICH·COTEL

HÆC·FACIES·HIC·CVLTVS·ERAT·CV·SEPTRA·TENE·
REX·αναβαριsωγ·SED·BREVE·TEPVS·EGO·
HENRICVS·ALDEGREVER·SVSATIE·FACIEBAT·
ANNO·M·D·XXXVI·
GOTTES·MACHT·IST·MYN·CRACHT·

Toward the end of the 18th century, which had for most of its duration been relatively free of fanaticism, a new messianic figure appeared—one who still has followers today. The Panacea Society of Bedford still claims to be in possession of the box of sealed writings left by Joanna Southcott, the "Bride of Christ," when she died in 1814.

This extraordinary woman was born in 1750 in a Devonshire village into a family of poor farmers. As a child she was very pious. One night, while in her teens, she had her first religious experience. She was sitting beside the bed of a dying man, a neighbor known for his atheism and suspected of having sold his soul to the Devil. Suddenly, the man sat up in bed and began raving that all the "black dogs of hell" were outside his window

Above: Bockelszoon and his deputies being tortured in the main square at Münster. It took more than a year for the forces sent to depose the Anabaptists to recapture Münster but after the city's fall their retribution was terrible. The Anabaptist leaders were exhibited in chains in a number of German towns before being returned to Münster to be publicly tortured to death.

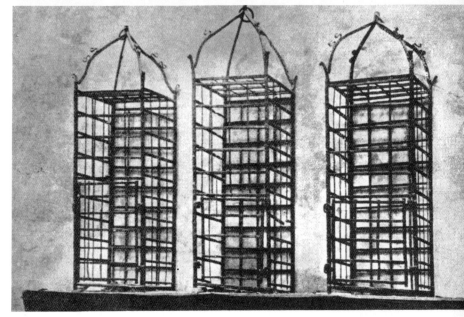

Right: in these iron cages, the mutilated remains of Bockelszoon and his two deputies were exhibited to the people of Münster as a warning against revolution.

Left: the prophetess Joanna Southcott. Joanna was over 40 when she first heard the supernatural voices that convinced her she had a divine mission to save souls. Thereafter, her teachings and prophecies gained her many followers, each of whom was saved by being "sealed" in the faith. Joanna sent each of the saved a certificate sealed with a seal she had found in the house of an employer: it bore the initials I.C., which Joanna interpreted as meaning Jesus Christ. Right: *The Imposter or Obstetric Dispute*, a satirical drawing published after Joanna Southcott had announced she was pregnant with the Second Messiah. Apart from her disciples, few believed that she was pregnant, and those who did asserted that the child's father was the Devil. Others thought Joanna mad. This scene is set outside "New Bethlem," a play on the name of the London madhouse, the Bethlem Hospital.

Right: Joanna Southcott's "box." According to tradition, at her death Joanna left a sealed box to be opened in time of national crisis. This particular box was sent to the National Laboratory of Psychical Research in 1927, and was opened by psychical researcher Harry Price in that year. The box undoubtedly belonged to Joanna, but it contained no instant solution for national emergencies.

and that he could already hear the "screams of the damned."

The young girl felt—as she later described it—"the pure strength of God flowing through [her] veins." Rising to her feet, she "exorcised the presence of evil," saying, "'Satan, I charge you by the Living Word of God to go hence and trouble this soul never again.'" The man fell back upon his pillow, apparently at peace, and died quietly toward morning.

As a young woman, Joanna Southcott moved to Exeter, where she worked as an upholsterer's assistant. There, she came under the spell of the Wesleyan movement, whose emotionally charged interpretation of the Gospels was then sweeping Britain. But it was not until she was into her 40s that this devout spinster began hearing a supernatural voice.

The voice, which called to her during the night, would be preceded by various raps on the wall, the windows, and the bed. Then the voice would address her: "Joanna Southcott, the Lord

God is awakening out of His sleep, and will terribly shake the earth. There shall be wars and rumours of wars. Nation shall rise against nation, and kingdom against kingdom. There shall be famines, and pestilences, and earthquakes. The sign of the Son of Man shall appear in heaven, and He shall come in the clouds with power and great glory. Watch therefore, for ye know not what hour your Lord doth come." The voice also commanded her to make these prophecies known to others.

Joanna dutifully wrote down the messages given to her and tried to spread the word. The Wesleyans refused to take her seriously. Then a skeptical but kindly Church of England vicar agreed to put her "voice" to a test. She wrote a message on a piece of paper, sealed it in an envelope, and marked the envelope "Open this at Christmas."

The following Christmas the clergyman opened the envelope and found inside it a prediction that the Bishop of Exeter would be dead by that time. At the time the message was written the Bishop had been in good health, but in December he had died.

Half convinced that Joanna did have some spiritual gift, the vicar suggested that she publish her writings. She followed his advice, borrowing the money for their publication, and in 1801 the first of her many books and pamphlets appeared under the title *The Strange Effects of Faith*.

Strange, certainly, were the events of the remainder of Joanna Southcott's life. She became convinced that she was the "second Eve"—the woman who would redeem mankind from the original sin into which the first Eve had led us. Christianity had already found a "second Eve" in the Virgin Mary, whose Son had brought

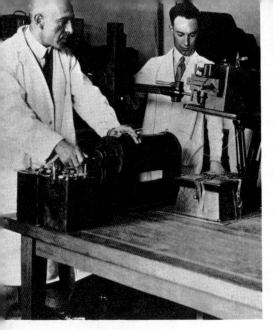

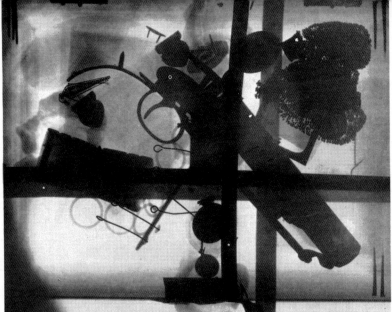

Above: Harry Price (left) with an assistant, about to x-ray Joanna Southcott's box. Joanna had stipulated that the box should be opened only in the presence of 24 bishops, and Price therefore decided to x-ray the box instead of opening it. Above right: Harry Price's x-ray of the contents of Joanna's box. Among the articles discernible in this photograph are a horse pistol, a dice box, and a purse containing coins. The contents also included a number of books, a lottery ticket, and a nightcap.

Below: the box Harry Price examined was not the only one left by Joanna; another belongs to the Panacea Society, who placed this advertisement in *Titbits* in 1954.

this redemption; but Joanna found passages in the Book of Revelation that seemed to refer to herself. She was the "woman clothed with the sun" who had the "moon under her feet, and upon her head a crown of 12 stars." Those who followed her would be the 144,000 elect spoken of in the Book of Revelation.

The political upheavals of the day—the French Revolution, followed by the Napoleonic Wars—added a measure of credibility to Joanna's doom-laden message, and after moving to London she soon acquired some 14,000 followers. Those who were "sealed" in the faith—that is, "saved"—received a certificate bearing the words "The Sealed of the Lord—the Elect-Precious Man's Redemption—To inherit the Tree of Life—To be made Heirs of God and Joint-Heirs with Jesus Christ." The elect were instructed to observe the Jewish Sabbath and to obey the dietary restrictions of the Old Testament.

Joanna continued to write and publish and to bombard clergy and Members of Parliament with her teachings. She prepared a sealed box supposedly containing special revelations, which was to be opened after her death by 24 bishops of the Church of England.

The circumstances of her death were both pathetic and grotesque. In her mid-60s, well past the menopause, she heard her "voice" announce: "This year . . . thou shalt bear a Son by the Power of the Most High." She published the good news in her *Third Book of Wonders*. The birth of Shiloh, the Second Messiah promised in Revelation, would take place on October 19, 1814. She invited the Prince Regent and other eminent people to send their personal physicians to verify this miraculous pregnancy. According to one of her biographers, a "leading surgeon of the day" said there was no doubt that she was pregnant, and this was confirmed by 17 of the 21 other doctors who examined her.

A sumptuous cradle was made for the expected Messiah. It was carved of satinwood and fitted with silk hangings, lamb's-wool blankets, and gold-embroidered sheets. As October 19 approached, crowds gathered outside Joanna Southcott's house. The day came and went. A new date was announced: December 24. She became ill. People worked themselves into a fever of

Above: Harry Price opening the
Southcott box he was sent in 1927.
Before opening the box, Price
wrote to three archbishops and 80
bishops to invite them to attend
the ceremony in accordance with
Joanna's wishes. In the event,
the only one present was the
Bishop of Grantham, who is seated
at the left of the platform.
Left: the actual contents of
the Southcott box opened by Price.
They were so mundane that
supporters of the Southcott myth
claim that Price's box was the
"wrong" one, and that another of
national importance still exists.

Above: Father Divine's "Throne Car." The center rear seat of the car was an elevated throne from which Divine could wave to the crowds and, at the touch of a button, a section of the roof slid back to show an enthroned "God." The car, especially built for Divine, was registered to "John the Baptist" of Beverly Hills.

excitement. Then, on December 27, Joanna Southcott died. The autopsy revealed a swollen condition of the womb.

Despite this blow to their expectations, many Southcott followers continued to believe in her divinity. They asserted that a "spiritual" child had been born and that one only needed the "eye of Faith to see and love Him."

Moreover, there was the sealed box, which was passed from one guardian to another as the years passed, with repeated urgings from the faithful that the Archbishop of Canterbury should open it. One box was certainly opened in 1927 and it was found to contain a few virtually illegible manuscripts, a woman's nightcap, and a lottery ticket.

Yet the Panacea Society continues to insist that the real box is still in its keeping.

Deluded she may have been, but at least Joanna Southcott was

Left: Father Divine rides through Harlem and the Bronx in his custom-built "Throne Car." Born George Baker, Divine began his career as assistant to an evangelical preacher, later opening a mission in Sayville, Long Island. He gave his followers free meals, and found them jobs—but in return expected them to contribute financially to the upkeep of "Heaven," as the mission was known. In 1930, Baker began to call himself Father Divine, and to claim that he was God.

Below: feasting played a very important part in the Divine cult, and huge meals were served to the faithful at the various Peace Missions. Two of Father Divine's followers said they had been converted to the cult by a meal consisting of fourteen different dishes, including two huge oval cakes "as large as automobile tires, but higher." But eating was the only sensual pleasure allowed to cult members: alcohol, tobacco, and sex were all taboo.

sincere and morally upright. The same cannot be said for some other claimants to divinity, such as Henry James Prince and his successor Smyth-Pigott, who used their supposed sanctity to lure trusting young women into bed with them.

Carrying on in the same tradition, but in a more flamboyant style, was George Baker, a black American who called himself Father Divine. He was born in 1880, the son of former slaves, on a rice plantation in South Carolina. He died in 1965, a millionaire, worshiped as God on earth. During the 1930s, when his cult was at its peak, its membership numbered hundreds of thousands (he claimed 20,000,000).

Early in his ministry, the young George Baker joined up for a few years with a Baltimore evangelist who called himself "Father Jehovia" and called Baker "The Messenger." Perhaps it was from Father Jehovia that Baker acquired a taste for messiahship. Anyway, by 1914 Baker had gone into business for himself, as it were, and was calling himself God. He attracted a huge following among blacks in Georgia, but antagonized the more orthodox black clergy and got into trouble with the law. In 1915 he was encouraged to leave Georgia, and he went to New York.

There were already a number of black missions in New York City, including one in Manhattan called the Church of the Living God. This was run by one of Baker's former associates called St. John The Vive Hickerson. Hickerson and his co-deities, the Temples of God, wore glittering crowns and proclaimed that they would never die.

Baker chose an unlikely location for his own mission, the mainly white community of Sayville, Long Island. By 1927 his flock still numbered only about 40. Membership began to increase when he invited people to partake of lavish free Sunday dinners. Before long, he had enlarged the scope of the mission to include an employment agency to help out-of-work members of the congregation to find jobs. The employed contributed most of their earnings to the upkeep of the Peace Mission in Sayville, which became known as "Heaven"—the first of many.

In 1930 George Baker was "reborn" as Father Divine. His ever-increasing flock readily accepted his divinity, and it is not hard to understand why. Although not physically imposing (he was only 5 feet 4 inches tall) he had great charisma. But more than this, he was their champion—at a time when blacks had few champions in either the North or the South. He fed them, found them jobs—and this during the Depression, when even whites were jobless and hungry—and told them they were "saved" and would never die. The heady feeling of being "special" that any cult gives its members was offered to them in abundance. The sect grew at an astonishing rate: by 1936 there were some 160 Peace Missions in the United States. Even some whites joined the movement.

Being saved by Father Divine was not just a matter of jobs and free meals. Disciples had certain responsibilities, and one of these was scrupulous honesty. "You're either honest or else you're dishonest," said Father Divine. "Keeping even a straight pin that does not belong to you is dishonest." He forbade his flock to accept government relief; and some converts who joined in later years insisted on repaying to the government the relief money they had drawn during the Depression. Like the Salvation Army, the Peace Missions attracted many repentant criminals.

As in most revivalist sects, alcohol and tobacco were proscribed. But that was not all. Sexual relations—even between husband and wife—were considered sinful and were forbidden. In the Peace Missions, the men and the women slept in separate dormitories. Their one sensual indulgence seems to have been food. The 20-course banquets at the Peace Missions were a glutton's idea of heaven, with tables piled high with hams, chickens, great mounds of ice cream, and cakes the size of beehives. During the banquets, disciples would confess their past sins and praise Father Divine for saving them. "I was a prostitute walking the streets," confessed one woman. "Now I meet Father and that holy man he give me new life. Father, you is wonderful, you is God."

Those outside the fold saw Father Divine in a different light. Generous he certainly was—but with whose money? His disciples were obliged to surrender 90 percent of their earnings to the communal fund; and of this money a sizable portion went to Father, enabling him to live in a style considered appropriate to God. He owned a fleet of automobiles, including the famous "Throne Car." This custom-built, 265-horsepower vehicle featured an elevated throne and a roof lined with white plush sprinkled with golden stars. At the touch of a button the top would open to reveal Father Divine on his throne.

Father Divine managed his money with extreme cunning, and despite the determined efforts of the Internal Revenue, he apparently never paid any income tax. This discrepancy between the rule of honesty imposed on his followers and the license to cheat that he allowed himself may have been paralleled by a double standard with regard to sex.

Married twice—the second time, at 66, to a 21-year-old Canadian girl—Father Divine always claimed that his marriages were purely "spiritual." There is no evidence to prove otherwise. However, the skeptical viewed with interest that fact that Father always surrounded himself with beautiful young girls, white and black, called Angels. Besides being decorative, the Angels served him as personal secretaries. But according to Faithful Mary, one of his protégées who had a falling out with Father, the Angels' duties were not purely secretarial.

Testifying in court in 1937, when Father Divine was on trial for ordering an attack on two process-servers, Faithful Mary painted a lurid picture of the goings on *chez* Father Divine:

"Up in the chambers of Divine at night with the lights low, Divine can be seen going through strange movements, while upon the floor lie several angels moving their bodies in sexual spasmodic jerks, disrobing themselves and some completely nude. They are hysterically crying out to him, and you can see that they are burning up and that the evangelical life is not in them."

That was Faithful Mary's story. But she had a grudge against Father, who had recently stripped away her power in the organization and taken back the lavish presents. Perhaps she concocted the account of Father's orgies. Two years later, she returned humbly to the fold and publicly confessed that she had

Above left: Father Divine with his second wife, Edna Ritchings, in 1946, the year of their marriage. At the time Divine was 66 years old, his bride only 21. Divine insisted that both his marriages were purely spiritual, to conform with the rule of his cult forbidding sexual intercourse, even between husband and wife. The youth and beauty of his second wife, however, gave skeptics ample reason to assert that his desires were very much those of the flesh.

Above right: Faithful Mary, one of Divine's disciples, accepts a Grand Jury subpoena to testify at Divine's trial. In 1937, Divine was charged with ordering an attack on two men trying to serve him with a writ. Mary, once the acknowledged female leader of Divine's cult, had fallen out with Divine and in her testimony accused him of holding sexual orgies with his young female followers—the Angels. No evidence was ever found to prove her claim.

Left: carrying a banner glorifying Father Divine, the Angels parade through Harlem to celebrate the founding of a "Heaven" in 1938.

lied. Her repentance did not suffice to win back her former privileges, however, and a few years later she opted out for a second time. She died of double pneumonia. "Retribution," said Father Divine.

He was prone to attribute the violent deaths of some of his opponents to their opposition to him. Comedian Will Rogers' death in an air crash was obviously caused by his making a joke about Father Divine shortly before the accident. Mussolini's execution in the last days of World War II was the result of his ignoring Father's demand that Italy relinquish control of Ethiopia.

The death of Father Divine himself was potentially most embarrassing for him and for his followers. Deaths within the sect had always been explained as the result of sin or secret disbelief on the part of the deceased. If a person died, it was proof that he was not truly saved. In Father's own case, this obviously could not be the explanation. So he announced from his deathbed that he was *not* dying. "I'm just dematerializing. If it takes a millennium I'll be repersonified in another body. I shall be back."

Messiahs have often turned up in non-Christian cultures. Islam, in particular, is a religion that has seen many messiahs, or mahdis, come and go. According to both the Shiite and the Sunni branches of Islam, the Mahdi will appear just before the Last Day and will abolish wickedness and bring about the triumph of Islam.

From the Islamic world, about 100 years ago, emerged a new messianic faith, an offshoot of Islam called Baha'i. Central to Baha'i is the belief in two recent manifestations of God: Mirza Ali Muhammad, called the Bab ("Gate"), and Mirza Hussein Ali, or Baha'u'llah ("the Glory of God"). The Bab began his

Above: Abdul-Baha, the supreme missionary of the Baha'i faith. Baha'i was founded in the 1840s by Mirza Ali Muhammad, known as the "Bab" or "Gate," who proclaimed the coming of a messiah, one even greater than the Bab. In 1863, Baha'u'llah proclaimed himself to be divine and took on the mantle of the Bab. It was he who propounded the important Baha'i doctrine of universal brotherhood and religious unity, but it was left to his son, Abdul-Baha, to spread his message through the whole world.

ministry in 1844 in the Persian city of Shiraz. He served as a kind of John the Baptist, preparing the way for the coming of Baha'u'llah; and yet in a sense, being himself divine, he was preparing the way for himself. The Bab and his followers, called Babis, were savagely persecuted by the Shah and by their Muslim compatriots. Finally, in 1850, the Bab was executed.

The story surrounding his execution confirmed his divinity in the eyes of the faithful. When summoned to go before the firing squad, the Bab was talking to his secretary. His reply to the prison official was: "Not until I have said to him all those things that I have to say can any earthly power silence me." Nevertheless, along with a young disciple who begged to share his fate, he was tied up in front of a firing squad of 750 riflemen.

When the smoke of the guns cleared away, the young disciple was found standing alive on the ground. Both ropes were severed. The Bab was nowhere to be seen. On witnessing this apparent miracle, the Armenian colonel who was in charge of the execution, and who had already half believed in the Bab, resigned his command. Eventually, the Bab was discovered back in his cell, talking to his secretary. When led away for the second time, he said, "I have finished my conversation with Said Hussein." This time, the rifle bullets hit their targets. According to the story, a violent dust storm covered the city for the rest of the day.

In 1863, Baha'u'llah proclaimed that he was the "Promised One" of all religions—not without some opposition from supporters of his half-brother Mirza Yahya, who had in fact been nominated by the Bab as his successor. For nearly 40 years Baha'u'llah lived as an exile and sometimes as a prisoner of hostile governments. He was hunted down several times by would-be assassins from Mirza Yahya. Yet even under these trying and often dangerous conditions Baha'u'llah still managed to give shape and purpose to the new religion. When he died in 1892, his son Abdul-Baha took up the task of propagating the faith. Soon Baha'i spread to the United States and then to Europe. It is in the United States that it has its greatest number of adherents in the West. Its headquarters are in Haifa, Israel, as the remains of the Bab and Abdul-Baha are buried on Mount Carmel, and Baha'u'llah is buried near Akka.

In essence, Baha'u'llah's message is the unity of all peoples and religions. According to the Baha'i faith, religious truth is progressive, not final, and in order to reveal His truth, God has manifested Himself several times in history. Earlier manifestations include Moses, Jesus, Zoroaster, Muhammad, and Buddha. Differences between one religion and another, according to Baha'is, can be attributed partly to misrepresentation on the part of the followers, but mainly to the relative immaturity of an evolving humanity. The coming of Baha'u'llah, they believe, was a sign that the time had come for humans to put aside their artificial divisions—social, religious, racial, national, linguistic—and become truly one people. Although the movement is based on the appearance of a messiah—or rather two messiahs—Baha'is are very concerned with humans and their relation to each other as well as with man's relation to God. Whether or not he was truly a messiah, Baha'u'llah certainly brought a message that would appeal to modern man.

Above: the Baha'i House of Worship in Wilmette, Illinois. Baha'i, a faith independent of race, nation, class, or creed, has found adherents in many Western countries, but its strongest following in the West is in the United States.

Left: Baha'is from all over the Americas assemble to witness the laying of the cornerstone of the first Baha'i temple in Latin America, in Panama City in 1968. Asians, Africans, and Europeans mingle with the peoples of the Americas, living proof of the Baha'i message of the brotherhood of man. In a world sickened by war and conflict, it is this doctrine of fellowship that gives the Baha'i faith its appeal.

6

West Meets East

Things have never been quite the same since the arrival of the Mahatmas. Their home was Tibet, according to Madame Helena Petrovna Blavatsky, who introduced them to the Western world in the 1870s, but they were not bound by the normal restrictions of time and space. They hovered unseen in the house in Adyar, near Madras, India, where Mme. Blavatsky established the headquarters of the Theosophical Society. Two of them, named Morya and Koot Hoomi, accompanied her wherever she went—their presence indicated by the sound of rappings and "astral bells." Many a convert to Theosophy was motivated primarily by a

Right: young American members of the International Society for Krishna Consciousness on the steps of the Washington Monument. In the United States and Britain, Krishna Consciousness has gained the Hindu god Krishna many new followers. These devotees, repelled by the self-seeking materialism of Western society, are finding happiness and peace in the age-old wisdom of the East.

ON THIS SITE IN FEDERAL HALL
APRIL 30 1789
GEORGE WASHINGTON
TOOK THE OATH AS THE FIRST PRESIDENT
OF THE UNITED STATES
OF AMERICA

"A collection of occult teachings revealed by the Mahatmas"

natural desire to make contact with these very mysterious beings.

The Theosophical Society was the first major attempt to bring Eastern philosophical and religious ideas into the consciousness of the West. It was founded in New York in 1875, in Mme. Blavatsky's apartment at 46 Irving Place. Her home had become a gathering place for those intrigued by magic, the new cult of Spiritualism (in which Mme. Blavatsky had acquired a reputation as a medium), and various kinds of occult knowledge. One of the foremost members of this group was Colonel Henry Steel Olcott, the devoted companion of H.P.B., as she was known to her friends, and an enthusiastic student of the occult. During one of H.P.B.'s gatherings, while a lecturer was expounding the influence of magical formulas on ancient architecture, Col. Olcott passed H.P.B. a note saying, "Would it not be a good thing to form a society for this kind of study?" H.P.B. nodded her agreement.

Not until the third meeting of the little society (whose original membership numbered 16) was the name "Theosophical Society" chosen. "Theosophy" means "divine wisdom" and had been applied in the past to the intuitive knowledge of God and the mystical perception of the oneness of human and divine nature, as experienced by mystics of both East and West. As developed by Mme. Blavatsky, who quickly became its leading exponent, Theosophy was a collection of occult teachings revealed by the Mahatmas. Foremost among these teachings was the belief that man was capable of evolving into a superior being through successive reincarnations and the building up of good *karma*. Karma in Hindu theology is the moral law, the belief that every action a person performs has moral significance and will influence his fate in future lives. The theory of evolution, which caused such consternation among religious people in the 1800s, was accepted by Theosophy, which added its own theory of *spiritual* evolution. Just as man had evolved from apelike creatures to reach his present state of physical and intellectual development, so he would further evolve in wisdom and the possession of occult powers. Some few people, according to H.P.B., had already achieved a high level of spiritual power and were graciously willing to help still-struggling humans along the path to enlightenment. These were the Mahatmas (the Hindu word means "great soul").

Capable of astonishing feats themselves—such as astral travel and materializations—the Mahatmas helped H.P.B. develop her own powers. Col. Olcott reported how she wrote her first major book, *Isis Unveiled*: "Her pen would be flying over the page, when she would suddenly stop, look into space with the vacant eye of the clairvoyant seer, shorten her vision as though to look at something held invisibly in the air before her, and begin copying on her paper what she saw. The quotation finished, her eyes would resume their natural expression. . . ." On one occasion, when she could not quite get a quotation right, she "apported" a couple of volumes into the room—presumably from the Mahatmas' library in Tibet.

The Colonel, who seems to have been rather a trusting soul, was obviously awestruck by H.P.B., and in this he was not alone. She was one of those people about whom it is impossible to be neutral. Many people reacted to her with aversion. In that supremely genteel age, Mme. Blavatsky's perpetual cigarette—not to mention her coarse language and violent rages—must have closed many doors to her. But there was no denying that this flamboyant Russian had a compelling personality, which many other people found irresistible. Her hypnotic blue eyes put people off their guard, and she spoke with absolute authority. If she was a fraud—and the evidence suggests that she was—she was certainly one of the most accomplished frauds in history. The subsequent success of the Theosophical movement, though due in part to the appeal of the teachings themselves, owed a lot to the forceful and cunning nature of its co-founder.

In the first few years, however, Theosophy made little pro-

Left: Madame Blavatsky, founder of the Theosophical Society. The society, the first major attempt to acquaint the West with Eastern thought, was founded in 1875 and is still active today. Its teaching is based on the concept of spiritual evolution common to many religions of the East.

Below, left and right: imaginary paintings of Mahatmas Koot and Morya Hoomi. According to Mme. Blavatsky, Mahatmas were Tibetan spirits who had already attained spiritual power, and would help others to do so. They accompanied Mme. Blavatsky wherever she went.

The Astral Voyager from Tibet

In 1956, the imagination of the West was caught by the appearance of an extraordinary book. *The Third Eye* purported to be the memoirs of a Tibetan monk-doctor-pilot, Tuesday Lobsang Rampa, and included many fascinating, apparently authentic details about Tibetan life. But a few academics engaged a detective to investigate the author. And he discovered that Rampa was none other than Cyril Hoskins of Rose Croft, Thames Ditton . . . England.

When taxed with his deception "Rampa" produced a curious explanation. Hoskins had once existed, but had swapped bodies with Rampa some years before. The Tibetan was adept at astral or out-of-body travel, so he met Hoskins to agree the changeover.

On June 13, 1949, so Rampa asserted, Hoskins was photographing an owl from a tree when a branch broke and he fell on his head. Suddenly he found himself floating above his body, attached to it by a silver astral cord. Toward him floated the astral form of Tuesday Lobsang Rampa—attached by an astral cord to his body in Tibet. Severing Hoskins's astral cord, Rampa took up residence in the Englishman's body, while the disembodied "astral" form of Hoskins disappeared.

gress. Perhaps Spiritualism siphoned off many of those who might otherwise have become members. At any rate, the Society's membership in 1878 had dwindled to almost nothing.

It was a natural development that the Colonel and H.P.B. should move to India and establish the new creed in its more fertile soil. Through an acquaintance, Olcott obtained an introduction to one Swami Dayananda Sarasvati, who had launched a movement called the Arya Samaj, dedicated to reforming the Hindu religion along the lines of the ancient Vedic writings. The Arya Samaj were favorably impressed with what they heard of Theosophy, and H.P.B., for her part, confided to Olcott that Dayananda was an Adept of the Himalayan Brotherhood, that is, an incarnation of one of the Mahatmas. It was decided that the two organizations should affiliate.

And so in 1879, having left the few remaining New York Theosophists to fend for themselves, H.P.B. and Olcott arrived in Bombay. They were welcomed enthusiastically by the Indians, who were delighted and surprised to meet Westerners who came not to impose their own religion on the natives but to learn the wisdom of the East. The Christian missionaries, not surprisingly, viewed the Theosophists' arrival as a distinct setback to their own efforts.

The two Theosophists traveled extensively in India, being entertained by swamis, rajahs, and English colonials, including newspaper editor A. P. Sinnett, who later became one of the leading lights of the London branch of the Theosophical Society. On a trip to Ceylon, they received an especially clamorous welcome. Swept up by the enthusiasm of the Buddhist Ceylonese, H.P.B. and the Colonel became Buddhists.

It was partly this conversion and partly a recognition that the Theosophists and the Hindu Arya Samaj differed in various other points as well that led to a split between the two groups. But even without the support of the Arya Samaj, Theosophy flourished. Within four years of the Westerners' arrival in India, they had established 100 branches throughout the country. They established new headquarters in Adyar, near Madras, in a splendid house set in extensive grounds. It is still today the headquarters of the Theosophical Society.

The most important room in the house was the Occult Room. It contained a curtained shrine, through which letters to the Mahatmas could be posted. The Mahatmas' replies were delivered in various ways. Some of them appeared in the shrine; others were "precipitated"—that is, they would suddenly fall from the ceiling or from the branches of trees. Some—however they originally arrived—were handed to the recipient by H.P.B. herself. One thing was certain: there was to be no communication with the Mahatmas bypassing H.P.B. On one occasion Sinnett and another English Theosophist named Hume, who were distressed by H.P.B.'s uncouth behavior, decided to try to establish a direct link with the chief of the Mahatmas, the Great Chohan. They wrote a letter to him saying that in order to spread the truths of Theosophy to the unenlightened, they must be able to work independently of H.P.B. Sinnett then handed the letter, as usual, to Madame Blavatsky for her to deposit in the shrine. A few moments later, she burst into the room where he was

Left: Henry Steel Olcott, one of the original members of the Theosophical Society and a life-long friend of Mme. Blavatsky. The society was founded in New York but in 1879, when American interest in Theosophy seemed to be waning, Mme. Blavatsky and Olcott went to India to start their cult in the land they considered the fountainhead of their beliefs. For this photograph, which was taken in Burdwan, Bengal, in 1883, Olcott even donned Indian dress.

Right: Swami Dayananda Sarasvati, founder of Arya Samaj (a movement dedicated to reform of the Hindu religion), was, according to Mme. Blavatsky, an incarnation of a Mahatma. While still in New York, Olcott was introduced to Dayananda and, as the Indian was impressed by Theosophy, it was agreed that the two organizations should be affiliated.

Below: the Theosophists gained so many followers in India that they were soon able to establish these splendid headquarters in Adyar.

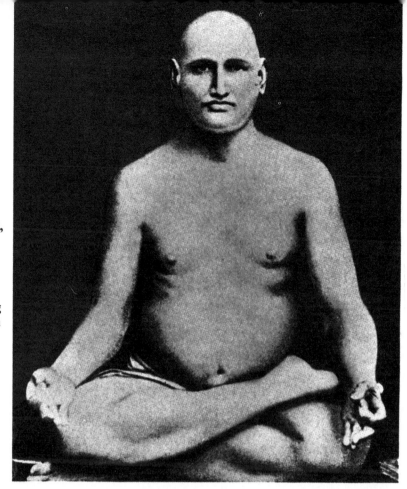

working, incoherent with rage. Sinnett went to get Hume, and the two men tried to calm her, but she was beside herself with anger. Apparently the faith of Hume and Sinnett in the Mahatmas was not drastically undermined by this incident. In fact, Sinnett carried the Theosophical message to England, and eventually he was blessed with more messages from the Mahatma Koot Hoomi, via Mrs. Laura Holloway, a visiting American medium. Shortly after H.P.B.—on a visit to London—heard of this development, Sinnett received another letter from Koot Hoomi, in which the Master disavowed any connection with the recent letters and warned Sinnett to approach him only through "the old woman." In John Symonds' entertaining biography *Madame Blavatsky* we learn that Sinnett "was convinced [the letter] was a fabrication of Madame Blavatsky's.... Sinnett was shocked to think that the Old Lady could do such a thing—take the Master's name and handwriting in vain." A bitter quarrel ensued, during which Sinnett nearly gave up Theosophy. In the end, he soldiered on.

While H.P.B. was in London being interviewed by the newly formed Society for Psychical Research, all was not well back at headquarters in Adyar. One of the people left in charge of the house, Madame Coulomb, had a grudge against H.P.B., who owed her some money. Madame Coulomb began to talk. She told certain of the faithful—and then the Christian missionaries —that there were no Mahatmas, and that her husband had been employed by Madame Blavatsky to construct certain trap doors for the purpose of "precipitating" the letters. In no time, the story was in print and the missionary papers were announcing with satisfaction "The Collapse of Koot Hoomi."

Worse was to follow. The Society for Psychical Research, who had been favorably impressed with H.P.B. and Theosophy, decided to send an astute investigator, Dr. Richard Hodgson, to have a look at Theosophy on its home ground. He arrived while H.P.B. and the Colonel were still away. He asked to see the shrine. Before admitting Hodgson to the Occult Room, some local Theosophists conferred and had a look at the shrine themselves. One of them struck it with his hand, saying, "You see, it's quite solid." Whereupon a panel in the back shot up to reveal a hole in the wall, on the other side of which was Madame Blavatsky's bedroom.

It was decided to remove the shrine. When at last Hodgson was shown into the Occult Room, the wall had been freshly plastered. But the former location of the shrine was obvious. The trap doors were attributed solely to the treacherous Coulombs; Madame Blavatsky, according to her supporters, had had nothing to do with them.

Hodgson interviewed various people and sent his report back to the S.P.R. He concluded that Madame Blavatsky was "neither . . . the mouthpiece of hidden seers, nor . . . a mere vulgar adventuress; we think that she has achieved a title to permanent remembrance as one of the most accomplished, ingenious, and interesting imposters of history."

After a brief return visit to India, punctuated by several clashes with the Coulombs, the press, and the missionaries, H.P.B. was persuaded by the faithful to leave India, for her own good and for the good of the Society. She spent her last few years

Left: A. P. Sinnett, British editor of an Indian newspaper, was one of India's leading converts to Theosophy. Tired of Mme. Blavatsky's methods, Sinnett and another Theosophist tried to communicate directly with the Mahatmas, but without success. This did nothing to impair Sinnett's belief in Theosophy, and he later returned to Britain to establish the movement there. Below: Mme. Blavatsky with Olcott in London, two years before her death. Although undoubtedly possessed of spiritual insight, she was not above the use of tricks to give the impression of spiritual power, and her death left unanswered the question: was she genuine, or was she a fraud?

Left: Annie Besant, who became leader of the Theosophists after the death of Mme. Blavatsky in 1891. She had joined the society only two years earlier, in 1889, a convert from atheism and a career devoted to social reform.

Nehru and the Theosophists

In 1947, India set sail as an independent state under the command of Prime Minister Jawaharlal Nehru. Nehru's role in the struggle to build up Indian nationalism and gain independence from Britain is part of history. But what is less well known is that, as a boy, he had been influenced by the ideas of the Theosophists.

Child of a wealthy patrician family, Nehru was educated at home until the age of 16 by a succession of English tutors. One of these, Ferdinand Brooks, was himself a Theosophist, and he took his young charge to a number of Theosophical meetings. At the age of 13, Nehru was initiated as a member of the movement in a ceremony conducted by Annie Besant, and as a member he attended the Theosophical Convention in Benares, where he saw Colonel Olcott.

According to Nehru, who in later life recorded his impressions of the Theosophists, he understood little of the metaphysical arguments at the meetings he attended, yet he was fascinated by the speakers and felt that he had found "the key to the secrets of the Universe." His encounter with the Theosophists made him think more seriously about religion, and he was deeply impressed by the *Upanishads* and the *Bhagavad Gita*, the great books of the Hindu faith. For, even though he came from a Hindu family, it was the Theosophists who introduced him to these works.

Soon after Brooks left the Nehru family, Jawaharlal was sent to school in England, and his contacts with the Theosophical Society lapsed. But many years later, this great man could still record that he felt he owed a debt to the Theosophist movement.

in Europe, writing another massive work, *The Secret Doctrine*. One of her compatriots, a man named Solov'yov, tried to get the truth about the Mahatmas from H.P.B. According to him, she finally confessed. "What is one to do," she said, "when, in order to rule men, you must deceive them, when, in order to catch them and make them pursue whatever it may be, it is necessary to promise and show them toys? Suppose my books and *The Theosophist* were 1000 times more interesting and serious, do you think that I would have anywhere to live and any degree of success, unless behind all this there stood 'phenomena'? I should have achieved absolutely nothing. . . ."

The discrediting of Madame Blavatsky by no means killed Theosophy. Many people, including such distinguished persons as Thomas Edison, W. B. Yeats, and Lord Tennyson, studied its teachings. In India Theosophy continued to grow in influence well into the 20th century, largely due to the tireless work of another woman, the English reformer Annie Besant. Ironically, many Indians first became acquainted with their own sacred writings, including the *Upanishads* and the *Bhagavad Gita*, by way of the Theosophical Society. Among these were two great Indian statesmen, Jawaharlal Nehru and Gandhi—whose title of respect, "Mahatma," had nothing to do with any supposed miraculous powers. Nehru, while in his teens, even belonged to the Society for a few years.

Today, the Theosophical Society has declined numerically. Its membership totals slightly more than 26,000, most of the members being in India, the United States, and Britain. In the meantime many other Eastern-inspired movements have swept through Europe and North America. One of the first of these—and still flourishing today—is Vedanta.

Vedanta means "the end of the Vedas"—that is, their reason for being, or their teaching. Vedanta was first introduced to the West in 1893 by a striking young Indian named Vivekananda. He had been sent by a rajah as a delegate to the Parliament of Religions at the Chicago Universal Exposition. Vivekananda arrived unannounced in Chicago two months before the opening of the Parliament, with a limited sum of money and no contacts. By the simple process of knocking on doors, he finally met someone who was able to introduce him to the Secretary of the Parliament.

When the Parliament finally opened, Vivekananda stole the show. He was clad in a long red robe, tied at the waist by an orange cord, and on his head he wore an imposing yellow turban. This costume had no official or religious significance—Vivekananda was not a priest but a disciple of the great mystic Ramakrishna. Nevertheless, he caused quite a stir. He was a spell-binding speaker. Many of his listeners did not quite grasp his meaning—and if they had grasped it, would doubtless have rejected it—but they were enthusiastic all the same.

Although based on the same writings as Hinduism, and related to it, Vedanta is quite distinct from Hinduism. In fact, its adherents tend to consider it a philosophy rather than a religion. In essence it is the belief in an all-pervading Reality (*not* a personal God) that is called Brahman when one is speaking of it as the Reality external to man and Atman when one is speaking of

Below: Annie Besant in 1926 with the young Indian Krishnamurti, whom she had proclaimed as a new Messiah. While still a boy, Krishnamurti was discovered by the Theosophists who, on investigation of his previous incarnations, found them to be particularly significant and indicative of mystical power. Brought up by the Theosophists, Krishnamurti later rejected Theosophy and became an independent and highly successful swami or religious teacher.

Right: Jawaharlal Nehru, first Prime Minister of independent India. As a young boy, Nehru was taken by his English tutor to several Theosophical meetings, which impressed him deeply. It was through these meetings that he came to value the Hindu religion and sacred books, the *Upanishads* and the *Bhagavad Gita*.

113

Left: the bronze statue erected
in Bombay to the memory of
Vivekananda, 19th-century prophet
of the Indian Vedanta religion,
and the man responsible for
introducing Vedanta to the West.
Vivekananda's very practical
message to his own people was one
of self-help. On his first visit
to the West, in 1893 as delegate
to the Chicago Parliament of
Religions, he conceived a great
admiration for the qualities
that had forged the prosperity
of the United States. Vivekananda
believed that although India
retained spiritual values lost
by the Americans, these were
worthless unless combined with
an attempt to improve the material well-being of the country's
huge population. So convincing
was his message that he managed
to raise huge sums of money in
the West to support the work of
his disciples at home, disciples
who were expected to work with
all their strength to improve
the living conditions of their
fellow countrymen, as well as
giving them spiritual help.

it as the Reality within man himself. The goal of life, according to Vedanta, is to discover the Atman within oneself and to realize one's unity with the Brahman.

Vivekananda's Chicago speeches were not, of course, the first introduction of the ideas of Vedanta to the West. Scholars in Europe and the United States had already discovered its ancient teachings. The American philosopher Ralph Waldo Emerson, for example, was influenced by them—in particular by the belief, held by several Asian religions, that the material world is an illusion, or *maya*.

But this was the first time that large groups of Americans heard the message direct from a practitioner of it. Vedanta was quickly taken up by some of the "top people" who had tired of Spiritualism. They wanted Vivekananda to cater to their spiritual needs on an exclusive basis. Vivekananda was no salon guru, however, but a serious missionary. He established a mission in an unfashionable street in New York and quickly attracted such crowds that people had to listen to him while sitting on the steps outside the house. He toured the United States, Canada, and England; then he returned to India where he established the Ramakrishna Mission to spread Vedanta in his own country.

Unlike many Indian spiritual leaders, Vivekananda believed firmly in the importance of material well-being. He had been dazzled by the prosperity he saw in the United States, and he was determined to rouse his Indian followers to work hard for the

good of themselves and their fellow men. "Indians, get off your backsides," was one of his rallying cries. He sent his followers out into the countryside to heal the sick and do manual labor—even including digging latrines. He had little patience with the self-contained spirituality that ignored the physical misery existing then—and now—in India.

On the other hand, he felt that the West could learn from India—that although it enjoyed material wealth it suffered from spiritual poverty. Many Westerners agreed with him, and some turned to Vedanta. By 1916 the Vedanta Society had branches in San Francisco, Los Angeles, Boston, Pittsburgh, Washington, and Connecticut, in addition to the original establishment in New York. Indian *swamis* (religious teachers) were invited to these

centers to guide students along the path toward higher states of consciousness and the ultimate goal of mystic union with the Atman-Brahman.

Along with the teachers of Vedanta came a host of assorted swamis, gurus, and yogis, some sincere, some phony, eager to exploit the new vogue for Indian mysticism. They soon found that one of the most popular forms of teaching was the physical and spiritual discipline called *Hatha Yoga*. There are several kinds of *yoga* (the Sanskrit word means "bridge," suggesting a bridge to self-discovery), including those of devotion (*Bhakti Yoga*), and intellectual exercise (*Raja Yoga*). But for most Westerners, "yoga" means Hatha Yoga. It is both a physical exercise and a mental discipline. Through the gradual mastering of its postures,

Left: Swami Bhagwan Shree Rajneesh, one of a number of Indian holy men who have chosen new ways to preach their message, either in the West or at home. To overcome the loneliness that assails someone meditating alone, Rajneesh holds sessions of mass meditation to help his followers upward on their spiritual path.
Right: Maharishi Yogi, better known in the West as Maharishi. Maharishi became famous when he acquired a number of celebrated disciples, among them British pop stars the Beatles and actress Mia Farrow. The flowers he holds are symbols of his message of love and peace; from these symbols grew the "flower power" cult of love and peace of the 1960s.
Below: 15-year-old Guru Mahariji arrives in Britain to be greeted by a crowd of disciples carrying flowers and playing drums and guitars. The teachings of the guru have made him rich, for the car in which he was driven away was a flower-covered Rolls-Royce, with his personal registration GM!

from the simple to the convoluted, the student gains control of his body, eventually to the point of controlling his breathing and thus calming his mind.

Hatha Yoga, like the other kinds of yoga, can be a means of experiencing union with the Brahman. It can also, according to some of its practitioners, be a means of eventually acquiring *siddhis*. These are extraordinary powers—we would say supernatural powers—such as turning base metals into gold, materializing and dematerializing objects, flying, and performing great feats of sexual endurance. Although the vast majority of yoga students probably aim no further than to achieve a serene mind in a sound body, and some few practitioners pursue spiritual enlightenment, a minority try to acquire siddhis.

An Indian cult that offers ways to acquire siddhis and that has achieved some popularity in the West is Tantrism. In sharp contrast to the puritanical nature of most Indian culture, Tantrism glorifies sex to the point of making it the principal way to attain spiritual enlightenment and salvation. In a land where women have traditionally been despised as lower than the lowest of the castes, the Tantrists idolize women. They give special veneration to the Hindu goddess Shakti, the personification of the Female Principle in the universe, whom they consider superior to her consort Shiva, the Male Principle. Much Tantric religious art includes representations of the *yoni* (female genitals), which are used as objects of meditation. Images of the *lingam* (phallus) in the yoni are also placed before the worshipers.

Tantric rituals often culminate with sexual intercourse between the worshipers, but this is arranged in a very impersonal manner. Individual desires are irrelevant; partners are sometimes drawn by lot. Some advanced Tantrists prefer that the partner be old or ugly in order to concentrate on the act itself, free from what they would consider extraneous aspects. Stripped of personal affection or desire, the act can bring the worshiper to an apprehension of ultimate reality.

Apart from this formalized ritual sex—called *maithuna*—Tantrists are encouraged to break society's sexual code as frequently and as outrageously as they like. Group sex, incest, and bizarre sexual practices are considered valuable in helping the person to transcend conventional ideas of good and evil. Also, sex even in its grosser forms—as distinguished from maithuna—can sometimes, according to Tantrism, yield spiritual insights.

This is the permissive form of Tantrism. There is also a restrictive form, in which the Tantrist disciplines himself to control his sexual energy. The man and woman will sleep in the same room, and eventually lie naked together, but without indulging in sexual intercourse. In retaining his semen, the male Tantrist can supposedly acquire siddhis.

Yoga—particularly Hatha Yoga—plays a large part in Tantrism, for the techniques of maithuna and of the symbolic intercourse demand a degree of muscular and breath control. Advanced Tantrists also follow disciplines to awaken the *kundalini*. The kundalini is a serpent that lies coiled near the base of the spine, in the lowest of the seven *chakras*, or focal points of the etheric body. Under the guidance of a guru, the Tantrist may learn the difficult and dangerous techniques of arousing the

Right: Tantric painting of the Cosmic Purusa with, at the top, the Hindu god Krishna with Radha and, at the base, Vishnu. Tantrism gave rise to an art of particular beauty and heavy with symbolism, in which the human body was often used as an analogy for the cosmos, or ordered universe. Purusa is the ultimate principle, pure spirit. Below: a Western pupil of Hatha Yoga practices one of its postures. Hatha Yoga is one of the most popular Eastern philosophies to have been introduced to the West, but many people practice it to achieve relaxation or bodily discipline, rather than as a physical path to a spiritual end.

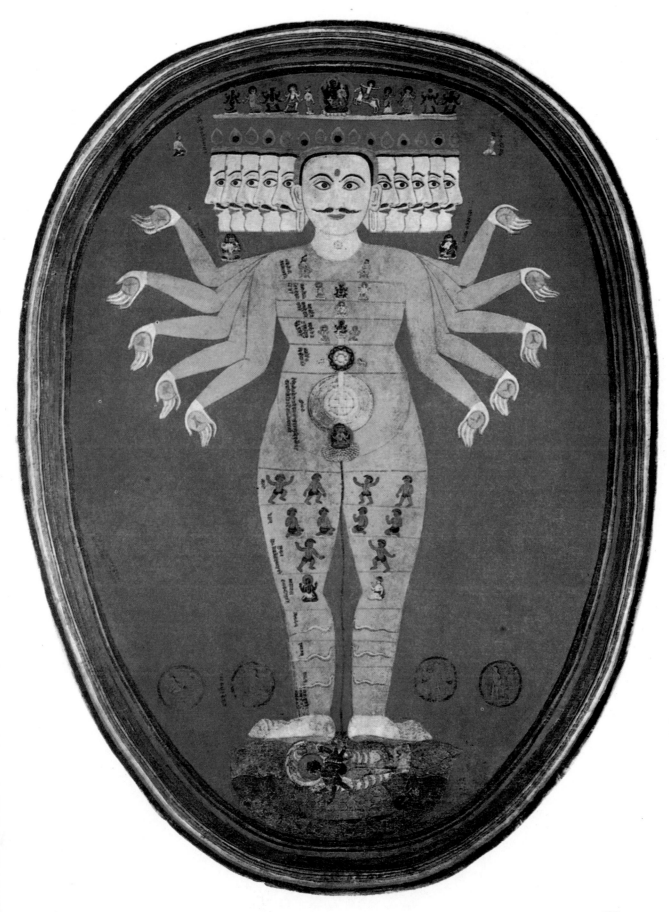

Above: Indian painting of the god Krishna with his especial beloved Radha on a terrace. To the Hindus, Krishna is a laughing god, and the source of all love. To the Krishna Consciousness sect, he is the sole deity, and through him alone can peace be achieved.

Right: Bhaktivedanta Swami Prabhupada, founder of Krishna Consciousness, at a meeting of the sect. The word *bhakti*, which is incorporated in the swami's name, means "loving devotion," and is the principal emotion associated with Krishna and his worship. Although the Krishna Consciousness movement was founded in India, and follows a Hindu god, it has never had much success there. The concept of Krishna as the one true god is alien to the Hindus, who worship many gods, including Brahma, Vishnu, and Shiva.

kundalini so that it ignites one chakra after another until it reaches the one at the crown of the head. At this point the person is suffused with bliss.

Tantrism *per se* is very much disapproved of by orthodox Hindus and is practiced by only a small minority in India and neighboring countries. But its influence lingers, particularly in certain yoga exercises (which Tantrists claim originated in their religion). Moreover, the beliefs of Tantrism have influenced occult movements in the West. The positive command to indulge one's sexual appetites and the possibility of working sexual magic were key principles of various cults, notably the Ordo Templi Orientis, which was founded at the beginning of this century in Germany.

Right: some disciples of Swami Prabhupada and Krishna Consciousness walk down New York's Fifth Avenue chanting their short mantra over and over again. Krishna Consciousness is a faith so simple that its members believe that inner peace can be achieved merely by the perpetual chanting of the words "Hare Krishna, Hare Krishna, Hare Rama Hare Hare Hare," and the simplicity of this belief is reflected in the disciples' simple lives.

At the other end of the spectrum from the permissive, magical, and complicated tenets of Tantrism is the wholesome and simplistic movement called Krishna Consciousness. These are the yellow-robed devotees who hop and chant "Hare Krishna" in city streets around the world. Krishna Consciousness is a new sect, but it is dedicated to a Hindu god who has been worshiped for many centuries.

Krishna is a pastoral god, normally depicted in Hindu art as a handsome young man. He has innumerable mistresses, chiefly milkmaids. He is described by one writer as the "universal protector and lover." The sacred book that tells the story of Krishna is the *Bhagavad Gita*, the treasured scripture of the Krishna Consciousness sect. Their leader is the Swami Prabhupada, an elderly man who claims to be the reincarnation of Krishna himself.

The Anglo-Indian writer Aubrey Menen describes Krishna Consciousness as "a faith of childlike simplicity." Its adherents—most of them young—live abstemious lives, practicing vegetarianism, avoiding drugs, indulging in sex only within marriage, owning no personal property. They believe that inner peace can be attained through the perpetual chanting of their mantra "Hare Krishna, Hare Krishna, Hare Rama Hare Hare Hare." They seem to be a happy group, unpreoccupied with complex philosophical questions and uninterested in the cultivation of magical powers—sexual or otherwise.

7

A Little Science...

"Cargo," to a Western ear, is a mundane sort of word associated with packing cases and freighters. But to some of the people of Melanesia, a group of islands in the South Pacific, the word "cargo" has connotations of magic. Ever since the Westerners began arriving in their great ships and, later, their astonishing flying machines, the islanders have been fascinated by the manufactured goods they brought with them. Canned foods, razor blades, refrigerators, china dishes, guns, and bottles of aspirin seem objects of mystery to people who have never seen a factory and have no conception of how such items are produced. The islanders

Right: healing the sick—with help from Venus. At such healing sessions in the chapel of the Aetherius Society in London's Fulham Road, variously colored lights are used to treat illness; green is supposed to be beneficial to those suffering from emotional troubles, circulatory and heart ailments, and headaches. The Aetherius Society, founded in 1956, is composed of disciples of the Master Aetherius, one of a superior race of beings who—according to the society—inhabit Venus and other planets. These Cosmic Masters watch over and protect earth through the Interplanetary Parliament, and hope to bring spiritual enlightenment to man.

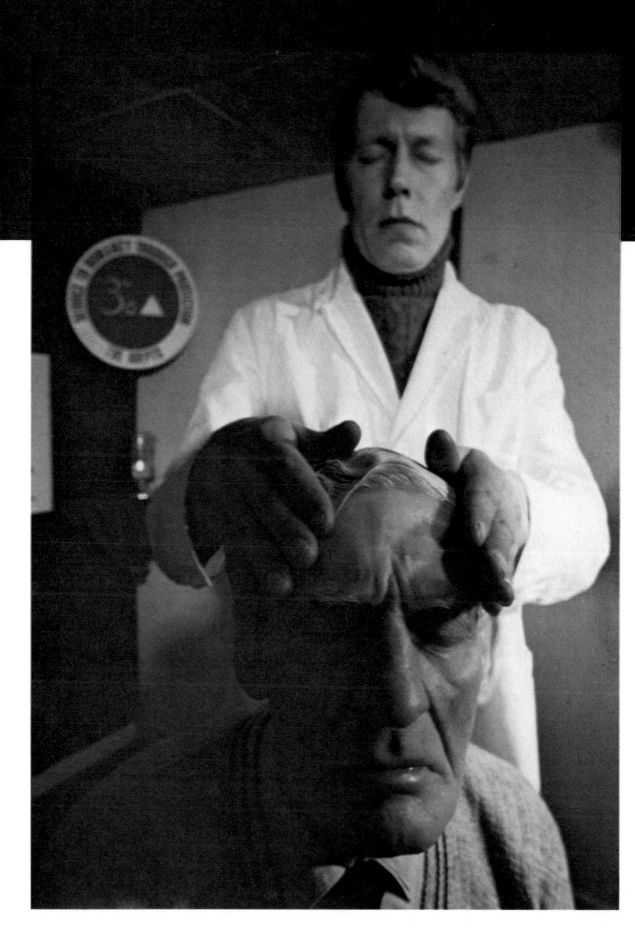

"The cargo is a spontaneous gift of the gods, intended to be shared by everyone"

believe that the objects are obtained by the white men by means of occult powers which they are too selfish to pass on to less prosperous people. Another belief is that the cargo is a spontaneous gift of the gods, intended to be shared by everyone, but that somehow the white men have claimed it for themselves.

The natives can obtain part of the cargo by the usual means of working for money with which to buy the items. Still, the belief lingers that someday a ship or plane loaded with free cargo for themselves will arrive—a gift from the gods. Occasionally this cargo myth is resurrected and developed into a cult by some prophet who announces that the end of the world is approaching. The prophet may tell the islanders that their ancestors will return on the ship bearing the cargo. He will direct them in various rituals and may order them to build a warehouse to store the goods and houses to accommodate the returned ancestors. Ceremonial washing, group sexual intercourse—or, in other cases, sexual abstinence—may be required by the leader as part of the preparation for the great day. In some cases, the cultists have pooled their money and tried to buy an important white leader, such as the President of the United States, in the belief that he possesses powerful magic that they too would possess if they owned him. It is not so much the manufactured goods themselves as their implication of power and the supposed superiority of the white man that gives rise to the natives' obsession with cargo.

When the expected millennium fails to occur, the discredited prophet may quietly go back where he came from, or he may try to explain why things went wrong. Life will resume its normal pattern and the cargo myth be half-forgotten. In time, another prophet will appear and another cult will form around his prophecy of cargo for all. Hopes will again be raised and dashed.

If you are tempted to smile at the naiveté of the Melanesian cargo cultists, consider the beliefs cherished by another group of people, called the Aetherians. These are not South Sea Islanders, but citizens of the technologically sophisticated West. Yet they, too, have visions of salvation by a superior race.

The members of the Aetherius Society are led by a man named George King, who in 1954 was washing dishes in his one-room apartment in London when all of a sudden a disembodied voice commanded: "Prepare yourself. You are to become the voice of the Interplanetary Parliament." Not long after this startling event, Dr. King was, in his own words, "overshadowed" by a being called the Master Aetherius, a Venusian who has since used Dr. King as a channel to bring spiritual upliftment to the world. Aetherius and the other delegates to the Interplanetary Parliament (which meets on Saturn) consider Dr. King their "primary terrestrial mental channel."

Taking his responsibility seriously, Dr. King rented a small lecture room in London's Caxton Hall for one evening early in 1955. The small audience on that occasion heard for the first time the voice of the Master Aetherius issuing from George King, warning them of the physical and spiritual danger in which earthmen were living. The message hit home; people returned to hear Aetherius again, and more people started attending, necessitating a larger meeting room. Today, the Aetherius Society has an international and expanding membership

Left: cargo cult votive board from the Nicobar Islands in the Indian Ocean. Cargo cults have arisen in various primitive island societies in response to the arrival of European travelers and European manufactured goods. The cultists, who know nothing of industry, believe that such goods are gifts from the gods that have been selfishly appropriated by the white man, and they hold to the dream of a day when the gods will give them a share of the cargo. This votive board depicts (in the center) a Nicobarese hut with an island canoe and a European ship, and (below it) the traditional riches of the islands—pigs and sea creatures. At the top, however, is a white man and the manufactured goods he has brought to the islands—the cargo wealth of which the cultists dream. Below: cargo cult shrine from the New Hebrides in the Pacific. The effigy is of Jon Frum, a white man who, the cultists believe, will bring cargo to the island in a huge scarlet plane. On the right is an image of the plane.

scattered throughout the English-speaking countries and other parts of the world. Communications from the Interplanetary Parliament are published in its magazine *Cosmic Voice*, and a large selection of books and cassette tapes on all aspects of Metaphysics.

The cosmic voice brings both good and bad news. Part of the good news is that Jesus is alive and living on Venus—one of the more advanced civilizations in our solar system. He has communicated again to mankind, through George King, and has given a new version of the Lord's Prayer, which includes a request for divine power. Recordings of the words of Jesus are spoken through Dr. King and are available from the Society. Although its members have a special reverence for Jesus, they regard him as only one of a number of Cosmic Masters who are helping man on earth—or Terra, as they call it.

The bad news is that man upon Terra is under constant threat from the forces of evil, mainly created by his own wrong thought and action. The Cosmic Masters, who in ancient times foresaw this present crisis, have gone to the limits of their power to help save and enlighten humanity. One of their main means of helping our endangered planet is a spaceship, one and a half

Left: Dr. George King, founder of the Aetherius Society, during the mission Operation Starlight. In this mission, Dr. King climbed 18 Mountains throughout the world, chosen by the Cosmic Masters. In each case, Dr. King was used as a human channel for the initial charge of spiritual energy put into these Mountains by Interplanetary Masters. This photograph shows Dr. King after the charge had been sent through him into one Mountain. Right: sound recording equipment in the Aetherius Society's headquarters in London is used to play recordings to the faithful of Dr. King's telepathic communications with the Cosmic Masters. Such a communication was responsible for the founding of the society. One day in 1954, while washing up, Dr. King heard a voice say: "Prepare yourself. You are to become the voice of the Interplanetary Parliament." Since then, the Masters' instructions to King have all been given by voices from outer space. Below: a group of Aetherius Society pilgrims on Holdstone Down in North Devonshire, England, during an organized pilgrimage. They are performing Holy Mantra and Prayer in order to release spiritual energy.

miles in length, called "Satellite Number Three." They bring this spaceship into a periodic orbit around earth and from it send massive quantities of *prana*, a vital energy known to practitioners of Yoga, onto the earth. This power, says the Aetherius Society, can be used by anyone who prays or acts unselfishly, and in Aetherius Society language the times when the Satellite is in orbit are known as a "spiritual push." "Satellite Three" is invisible and unable to be detected by radar. During such periods, the members of the Aetherius Society contribute to the spiritual push by means of certain prayers, meditations, and other spiritual exercises.

From 1958 to 1961 Dr. King was engaged in a major—and hazardous—project called "Operation Starlight." The initial charge of energy, says the Aetherius Society, was sent into 18 mountains around earth by a Cosmic Master through Dr. King, and afterward a massive amount of energy flowed into these New Age Power Centers, making them holy places. It can be released by *anyone* who goes to the Mountains to pray for world peace and enlightenment. The project took Dr. King and a few followers from Britain to the western and northern ranges of the United States, to Australia, New Zealand, France, and Switzerland. Most of them were inexperienced climbers, but that did not deter them from attempting such imposing peaks as Mt. Baldy (10,000 feet) in California and Castle Peak (14,000 feet) in Colorado. The last mountain chosen by the Masters was Mount

Below: Dr. King performing Tibetan Mudra Yoga during the American inauguration of the mission Operation Prayer Power in the Utah Desert in September 1973. He is directing the spiritual energy, invoked by the Mantra Team, into the battery, where it is stored to be released at a future date.

Kilimanjaro (19,000 feet) in Tanzania, which was charged through a Member of the Terrestrial Hierarchy of Ascended Masters—the Great White Brotherhood.

Since 1961, many other vital, difficult tasks have been performed by Dr. King and the Aetherius Society under the direction of the Cosmic Masters. Since 1954 Dr. King has acted as the channel for 592 Cosmic Transmissions—and the Aetherius Society claims this as a world record.

The Aetherius Society is a product of the "flying saucer" craze that developed shortly after World War II. Suspected at first—by the U.S. Air Force at least—of being a new development in Soviet aircraft, the unidentified flying objects were quickly identified by some people as visiting spacecraft from other planets. The widespread eagerness to believe in this theory is examined by Dr. Christopher Evans in his book *Cults of Unreason*. He observes that "powerful emotional factors" are at work in this situation, and sums them up as follows: "The God of orthodox religion has been found wanting . . . and can no longer be relied upon when Man is in dire circumstances. In his place new Gods have arisen—superintelligent beings who are technologically and, perhaps, morally superior to mankind. They come not from some outdated Dantean Heaven, but from one or many of the myriad planets which undoubtedly exist in the vast arena of the universe. They no longer ride on clouds or chariots of fire, but in fast and manoeuvrable spaceships of a

Below: members of the Aetherius Society study charts of the Pacific Ocean, prior to setting out on Operation Bluewater. During this mission, Dr. King was instructed to assist in the charge of a Psychic Center of the earth, situated just off the coast of California, with spiritual energy.

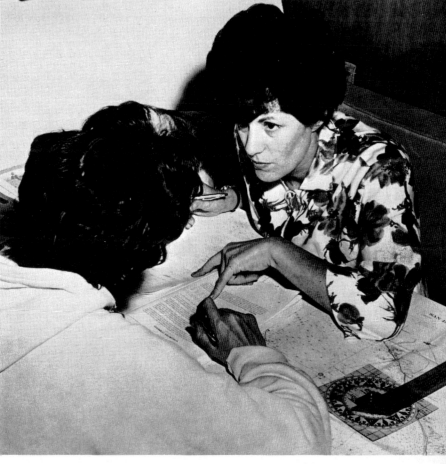

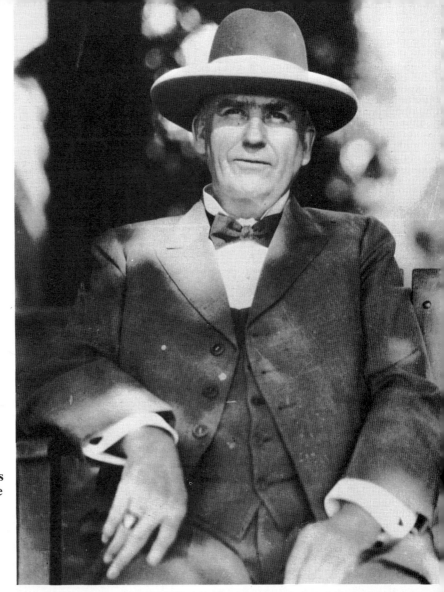

Right: Wilbur Glenn Voliva, founder of the Christian Apostolic Church of Zion, Illinois, in about 1929. Like the religious authorities of the Middle Ages, the Christian Apostolic Church holds fast to the Biblical statement that the earth is flat, not round.

Below: fire destroys the Shiloh Tabernacle of the Christian Apostolic Church in Zion in 1937. As technology and communications have advanced, it has become more difficult for members of the Christian Apostolic Church to keep to their beliefs. For who, seeing a photograph of the earth taken from space, could persist in maintaining that it was flat?

bewildering variety of designs, most commonly shaped like giant inverted saucers."

An illustration of this will to believe in visitors from outer space is the recent spectacular success of Erich von Däniken's books, such as *Chariots of the Gods?*, which purport to show that the great achievements of ancient civilizations, such as the pyramids, were really accomplished by a superior race of men from another planet. Although archaeologists and other scientists have pointed out many flaws in reasoning, as well as simple errors of fact, in von Däniken's books, their sober arguments have slight appeal compared to the tingle of excitement generated by the thought of supermen from "out there." A sort of collective feeling of inferiority is implicit in this attitude. When we consider the readiness of von Daniken's fans to deny that our ancestors—mere earthmen—were capable of building the pyramids, or the reliance of the Aetherians on spiritual guidance from Venus, the Melanesian cargo cultists' exaggerated awe of Western man and his technology does not seem quite so eccentric.

Our own familiar planet has provided plenty of material for speculation among amateur scientists and has given rise to many pseudo-scientific cults. For the past several hundred years, geographers, geologists, and astronomers have been finding answers to questions about earth and its formation, and by now we have a fairly complete scientific dossier on our planet. Yet there are always some people who prefer to reject the scientifically orthodox view in favor of deviant theories.

One would have thought, for example, that the theory that the earth is a sphere had long ago been proved to everyone's satisfaction. Yet for the few remaining members of the Christian Apostolic Church in Zion, whose members live in the little town of Zion, Illinois, the world is flat. In the early part of this century, Zion was a thriving community, rigidly puritanical, led by a man named Wilbur Glenn Voliva. Like other fundamentalist sects the Christian Apostolic Church maintained that the Bible is literally true, and they found in its pages many statements which, if taken literally, support the idea of a flat earth. To these Biblical "proofs" Voliva added his own homespun geology and astronomy. In the center of the flat earth was the North Pole; around its circumference was distributed the South "Pole"—a ridge of snow and ice to prevent ships falling off the edge.

He viewed with contempt modern discoveries about the sun. "The idea of a sun millions of miles in diameter and 91,000,000 miles away is silly. The sun is only 32 miles across and not more than 3000 miles from the earth. It stands to reason it must be so. God made the sun to light the earth, and therefore must have placed it close to the task it was designed to do. What would you think of a man who built a house in Zion and put the lamp to light it in Kenosha, Wisconsin?" (Laughter and applause.)

Other amateur geophysicists devised more imaginative theories. In the late 19th century an American named Cyrus Reed Teed, who called himself "Koresh," advanced a complicated theory that the earth is hollow and that we are living on the inside of it. At the center of this hollow space, according to Teed, is a sun, half light and half dark, of which we can see only a reflection. The rotation of the real sun gives us the phenomena of night and

Above: the radio station at Zion, Illinois, from which Voliva broadcast his beliefs. He not only maintained that the earth was flat, but also asserted that the sun was only 32 miles in diameter, instead of 864,000 miles, and not more than 3000 miles from earth, instead of 93 million miles!

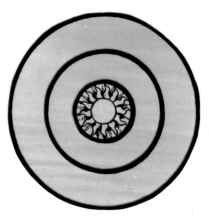 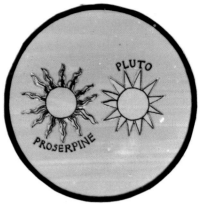 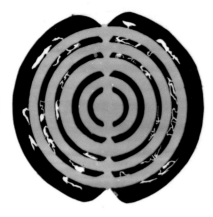

Above: 17th-century astronomer Edmund Halley saw the earth as three hollow shells around a sun.

Above: in the 19th century, John Leslie drew the earth as a skin within which two suns revolved.

Above: expanding Halley's theory, John Symmes suggested the earth shells were open at the poles.

Below: drawing of the world made in the 6th century A.D. Early Christian geographers based their theories on the Bible, rather than on scientific observation. This "map" depicts the earth as a rectangular box—the Tabernacle of Moses—the lid of which forms the sky. Within the box, ocean surrounds the earth mountain, over which the sun rises and sets.

day. The other heavenly bodies, he explained, are not solid objects, but tricks of the light. Like the apparent convexity of the earth, they are essentially an optical illusion. The density of the atmosphere was Teed's explanation for our inability to see the other side of the hollow shell in which we live.

These truths had been revealed to Teed by a beautiful woman who suddenly appeared to him one night as he was practicing alchemy in his laboratory. He published an account of this experience entitled *The Illumination of Koresh: Marvelous Experience of the Great Alchemist at Utica, N.Y.* The wording of this title suggests the delusions of grandeur that Teed shared

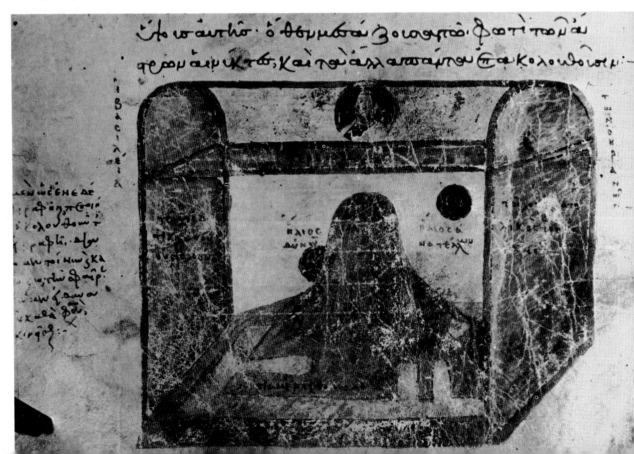

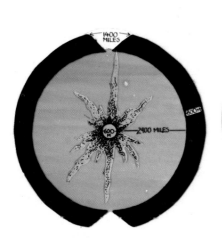

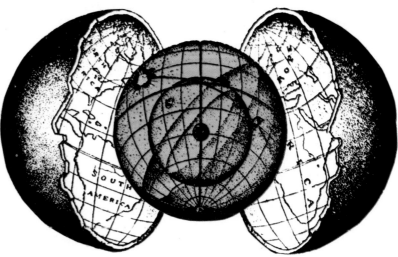

Above: in 1914 Marshall Gardner combined earlier theories in a sun-centered earth open at either end.

Above: American Cyrus Reed Teed conceived one of the strangest hollow earth theories, saying that man lives on the *inside* of a concave earth that contains the sun, the moon, and the stars.

with other prophets of pseudo-science. They tend to compare themselves with misunderstood original thinkers of the past, such as Galileo, and to attack orthodox scientists as "quacks." In his book *The Cellular Cosmogony*, Koresh declared ". . . to know of the earth's concavity . . . is to know God, while to believe in the earth's convexity is to deny Him and all his works. All that is opposed to Koreshanity is antichrist."

In Chicago, where he settled in 1886, Teed established the headquarters of the new faith. He published a periodical called *The Guiding Star*, later to become the more militant-sounding *Flaming Sword*. By 1894, according to *The Chicago Herald*, the cult had 4000 members, three quarters of them women. Koresh had the "mesmerizing" eyes typical of the successful cult leader, but did not succeed in mesmerizing his wife, who soon left him.

Having earned large sums of money through his preaching ($60,000 in California alone), Teed was able to found his own colony, called Estero, on a tract of land on the Florida Gulf coast. He confidently expected an eventual population of 8,000,000 for Estero. Only 200 believers arrived.

Koresh died in 1908, but his cult continued into the 1940s. *The Flaming Sword* was still being published in 1949, until a fire in the Estero printing plant put an end to the operation. No doubt a few Koreshans are still alive today. It would be interesting to hear their reactions to the photos of our convex earth taken by the astronauts.

Although Koreshanity never advanced beyond the credo of a small minority, another eccentric cosmological theory received official support from a powerful government, that of Nazi Germany.

Hanns Hörbiger was an Austrian engineer who, while in his 30s, had a vision that gave him a clue to the universe: Cosmic Ice. In 1912 he published a 790-page tome entitled *Glazial-Kosmogonie*. It was filled with elaborate diagrams and photographs that allegedly showed how the universe had been formed—and was still being formed—by the interaction of hot metallic stars and H_2O "in its cosmic form," namely ice. A collision

Left: Hanns Hörbiger, Austrian propounder of the Cosmic Ice theory. According to this theory, the universe has been formed by collisions between hot stars and gases such as hydrogen and oxygen in their "cosmic form," ice. A kind of "cosmic" gravity within the universe attracts all the bodies in each stellar system toward a central sun. Smaller bodies are captured by larger ones, and become satellites or moons, but as cosmic gravity constantly draws moon and planet closer, a disastrous collision between the two eventually results. Right: idealized statue of a German Bronze Age woman, from a book by Hörbiger. His theory provided an extremely convenient explanation for the disappearance of the "lost" city of Atlantis, where many Germans believed that the Aryan "master race" had originated. Hörbiger therefore became a prophet to the Germans, particularly the Völkisch cults. Far right: a German Bronze Age man, also from Hörbiger's book.

between this Cosmic Ice and a hot star, according to Hörbiger, produced a stellar system. Within such a system, bodies moved in a spiral toward a central sun, and on their way captured smaller bodies. Our earth, it seemed, had thus acquired several previous moons and would someday be struck by our present moon, which was moving closer all the time.

An English disciple of Hörbiger, named Bellamy, wrote an alarming account of how the last moon closed in upon our planet. As it came closer to earth it moved faster and faster, until it was circling the earth six times a day, its great pitted face eclipsing the sun three times a day, terrifying our ancestors. According to Bellamy, it was the sight of this menacing object that gave rise to legends of dragons and flying monsters and to the "Devil" of Hebrew-Christian folklore. The moon pulled the oceans into a "girdle tide" around the equator and twisted the earth out of shape. When, finally, the moon disintegrated, it fell onto the earth in a deluge of rocks, causing earthquakes, volcanic activity, and the great flood described in the Bible.

In Germany, Hörbiger's Cosmic Ice theory attracted fanatical support. Popularized versions of the complex doctrine were published in book and pamphlet form. Cosmic Ice devotees would attend scientific meetings and heckle the speaker, shouting "Down with astronomical orthodoxy! Give us Hörbiger!"

Hörbiger's theory of the moons crashing into the earth found favor with enthusiasts of the Atlantis myth, who found it a convenient explanation for the disappearance of this legendary continent. In Germany Atlantis was widely considered to have

Right: Mexican step pyramid lashed by a tidal wave, from a book by Hanns Hörbiger. Hörbiger believed that the early civilizations of Europe and the Americas were founded by colonists from Atlantis who introduced such arts as pyramid building to their new homes. When Atlantis disappeared in the cataclysmic collision between earth and moon, a huge tidal wave swept over its colonies, but the colonists took refuge in their pyramids, above the water's reach.

been the home of the original Aryan "master race." Thus, a sort of cross-fertilization of mythologies took place among people inclined to the occult.

The ideas of Hörbiger were taken up by one of the leading Nazis, Heinrich Himmler, and by the Führer himself. Hitler announced that when he built his ideal city at his birthplace, Linz, Austria, he would have an observatory built there and dedicated to Hörbiger. A Nazi pamphlet on Cosmic Ice proclaimed that it provided a truly Germanic scientific world view.

In spite of its close identification with Nazism, Cosmic Ice attracted people of different political persuasion, and it remained popular in England, thanks largely to Bellamy's writings, until well after the Second World War. Recently its supporters have tended to remain silent—perhaps in reaction to the on-the-spot discoveries about the moon.

As we have seen, a strong streak of megalomania runs through the histories of the founders of crank scientific cults, together with a tendency to paranoia. It would be hard to find a more extreme example than the case of Alfred William Lawson, Supreme Head and First Knowlegian of the University of Lawsonomy, Des Moines, Iowa. A blurb on Lawson's book *Manlife* (published by Lawson himself in 1923) proclaims: "In comparison to Lawson's Law of Penetrability and Zig-Zag-and-Swirl movement, Newton's law of gravitation is but a primer lesson, and the lessons of Copernicus and Galileo are but infinitesimal grains of knowledge."

Born in London in 1869, Lawson moved to the United States with his parents while still a child. In adulthood he went into the young aircraft manufacturing industry, and was fairly successful at it. Soon, however, he began to turn his mind to more profound matters. A preface to *Manlife*, written by one Cy Q. Faunce (probably a pseudonym for Lawson), rhapsodizes: "There seems to be no limit to the depth of his mental activities . . . countless human minds will be strengthened and kept busy for thousands of years developing the limitless branches that emanate from the trunk and roots of the greatest tree of wisdom ever nurtured by the human race."

Lawsonomy is nothing if not comprehensive; Lawson defined it as "The knowledge of Life and everything pertaining thereto." One of its basic concepts is that there is no such thing as energy, but that all movement in the universe is caused by suction and pressure exerted on one substance by another. Light and sound, according to Lawson, are substances drawn by suction into the eye and ear respectively. The earth itself is busily engaged in suction and pressure; at the North Pole, nourishing substances from the atmosphere are sucked into an opening, then fed through a system of arteries to all parts of the earth. Waste particles are flushed away along other passages and eventually expelled through the South Pole.

Another key Lawson concept is that of the Menorgs and the Disorgs. These are little creatures that live in the human brain. The *Menorgs* ("mental organizers") are responsible for all constructive activity, mental and physical. Constantly challenging and occasionally thwarting the efforts of the Menorgs are the malicious *Disorgs* ("disorganizers"). A hymn sung by Lawson's followers contains this stirring stanza:

"Menorgs are wondrous builders all,
Builders of the great and small.
All of life they permeate,
All formations they create.
Disorgs tear down eternally
While menorgs build faithfully."

Lawson's popularity dates from the early years of the Depression, when he founded a cult for economic reform called the Direct Credits Society. Thousands of people who were bewildered, frightened, and angry at the disaster that had hit them turned with pathetic enthusiasm to Lawson's facile economic theories. One of his proposals was that valueless money should be issued and all interest on debts canceled. This would rid the world of the financiers—"pig-like maniacs," Lawson called them—who had caused all the trouble.

Tens of thousands of people joined the Direct Credits Society. They held parades and mass meetings to celebrate Lawson ("God's Gift to Man") and his wisdom. One meeting in Detroit's Olympia Auditorium was attended by 16,000 people, who gave their leader a 15-minute ovation.

Having strong ideas on education, Lawson founded his own university. In 1942 he purchased the buildings formerly used by the defunct University of Des Moines, and began teaching a curriculum based exclusively on his own writings. By 1952 the University of Lawsonomy had some 20 students, all men, who studied there free of charge, working part-time on various agricultural and engineering projects. In 1954, after being investigated for tax evasion by a Congressional committee, Lawson sold his university for $250,000 to a businessman who planned to turn it into a shopping center.

By this time, Lawson had developed a full-blown case of the paranoia that so often afflicts the self-proclaimed genius. In *Fads and Fallacies in the Name of Science*, first published in 1952, Martin Gander described Lawson's apparent state of mind in his old age: "He feels himself surrounded by treacherous enemies. They are waiting for him to die so they can seize the holdings of his organizations. In recent years the conviction that he is a prophet of the Lord has increased ominously."

Lawson died in 1954 in San Antonio, Texas. His various enterprises were by that time combined in an organization called the Humanity Benefactor Foundation, Inc., based in Detroit. Recent inquiries to their address have brought no response from the foundation, so presumably the principles of Lawsonomy have suffered a sharp decline in popularity.

Modern science and technology have produced a profusion of miracles. Of course they are not really miracles, but to the layman they often seem so. The computer, the laser beam, the splitting of the atom, are for most of us mysterious phenomena that we accept because they obviously exist but that we do not really understand.

Perhaps it is not so surprising that many people are prepared to believe not only in the miracles of orthodox science but also in the miracles promised by the maverick or crank scientist. This is particularly true in the case of gadgets. "To most people," writes Christopher Evans, "any bit of technical apparatus, provided that it has a wheel turning, a light flashing or a needle wagging, is immediately exciting and somehow convincing on its own." Several modern cults have made use of existing machines to lend an aura of scientific validity to their teachings. The members of the "feedback churches," who measure and try to control their brain waves by means of the electroencephalograph, are a good example. Informal cults—in the loose sense of the world—have grown up around other "black boxes," particularly as they relate, or supposedly relate, to the diagnosis and treatment of disease.

Dr. Albert Abrams, a physician who practiced in California in the early years of this century, began at one point in his career to

Above: Dr. Albert Abrams with his oscilloclast. Abrams conceived his machine as a panacea that would harmonize all the disharmonious electronic oscillations of the body by which he believed all disease was caused. Right: how to operate Abrams' dynamizer. The specimen caused vibrations in the body, from which the disease could be diagnosed.

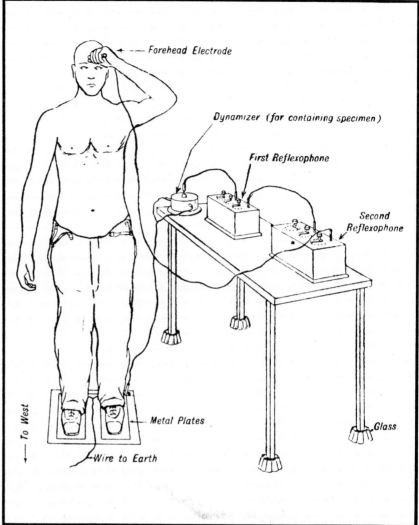

Forehead Electrode

Dynamizer (for containing specimen)

First Reflexophone

Second Reflexophone

To West

Metal Plates

Glass

Wire to Earth

diagnose illness by tapping the patient on the abdomen. Then he devised a machine, which he called a "dynamizer," to help in the diagnosis. This was a box with a tangle of wires inside, one of them connected to a battery. A blood sample from the sick person was put on some blotting paper and placed inside the box. Then a wire from the box was attached to the forehead of a healthy person—who for some reason was required to face west. The doctor would tap the abdomen of the healthy person. The theory was that "vibrations" from the blood sample were somehow amplified by the "dynamizer," and transmitted through the body of the healthy person, and could then be analyzed by the doctor.

But this was only one of the dynamizer's uses. It could also detect psychological disturbances; it could identify the person's age, sex, and religion. If a blood sample was not available, a sample of the person's handwriting would do.

Fired with his supposed success, Abrams built another machine—this one for the treatment of disease—which he called an "oscilloclast." It, too, operated by means of "vibrations." Yet another machine, called the "reflexophone," could diagnose illness over the telephone. Abrams constructed duplicates of his

marvelous machines and rented them out to quack doctors all over the country. Income from these rentals, and from the courses and lectures he gave to his numerous admirers and disciples, made Abrams a millionaire twice over.

In recent years, another pseudo-medical gadget, the orgone box, has attracted widespread enthusiasm. This, too, was devised by a man with genuine medical training, Dr. Wilhelm Reich. One of Freud's early disciples, Reich made significant contributions in the field of psychoanalysis. During the 1920s and 1930s his ideas were almost as influential as Freud's, and his books on psychoanalysis, notably *Character Analysis*, are still read and admired today. Even more strongly than Freud, Reich held that sex was the basic motivating factor in human behavior. He maintained that the orgasm itself had positive physical effects over and above its contributions to one's sense of well-being. He came to believe that a kind of life energy, which he called *orgone* energy, was concentrated in the genitals during the orgasm, then flowed gently back into other parts of the body. Thus the orgasm ensured the healthy functioning of the body as a whole, as well as a healthy state of mind.

Reich took this idea further and further. Orgone, he discovered, is blue in color, comes from the sun, and is found in air, water, and all organic matter. In 1940 Reich invented the Orgone Accumulator. This is a simple-looking box, about three feet square, consisting of two layers: an outer layer of wood to attract orgone energy, and an inner layer of metal that, unable to hold orgone itself, reflects it onto the person sitting inside the box. Over a certain period of time, the amount of orgone that is accumulated and radiated inside the box reaches very high, and supposedly therapeutic, levels.

Reich's Institute of Orgonomy, located on Long Island, New York, also developed other orgone-focusing gadgets, such as special blankets and small boxes for local application. According to its discoverer, orgone energy is useful in the treatment of such illnesses as anemia, hay fever, arthritis, certain types of migraine, chronic ulcers, and cancer in its early stages (except for tumors of the brain or liver).

Not surprisingly, these startling claims quickly received enthusiastic support from thousands of people suffering from these and other illnesses who had had no success with conventional medical treatment and were convinced orgone energy would make them well. They also received outspoken criticism and occasionally derision from the medical profession. Criticism had its usual effect in such cases: it intensified Reich's fanaticism. He wrote a book entitled *Listen Little Man!* in which he berated and derided the people who failed to recognize his genius, called them "cackling hens," and compared himself to a "lonely eagle" able to "detect new worlds, new thoughts, and new forms of living."

He continued to announce new ramifications of the orgone theory. Our earth, it seemed, was the center of an inter-galactic war, in which orgone energy was the booty. Hostile flying saucers were engaged in robbing us of our orgone energy, while friendly ones replaced it. He reinterpreted religion in terms of orgone: Christ, he claimed, was in direct communication with the cosmic orgone forces. "The science of Orgonomy," concludes Paul A. Robinson in his book *The Sexual Radicals*, "was as fantastic and elaborate as any theological system, and its content was identical with that of the great religions of salvation: it promised both a total interpretation of reality and a total therapy for man's individual and social ills."

Appropriately, Reich died a martyr's death. In 1950, the U.S. Food and Drug Administration obtained an injunction against him for selling and renting his orgone accumulators through the mails. Reich disregarded the injunction. Eventually, he was brought to trial, fined $10,000, and sentenced to two years in jail. He died in the Federal Penitentiary in Lewisburg, Pennsylvania, in 1957, aged 65, after serving less than half his sentence.

Yet Reich and his ideas continue to gain converts. Some of these followers take a Spiritualist approach, sitting in blue robes and communicating with the departed master by means of a ouija board. Lately, he has been taken up by the hippies, who find that his sexual teachings accord well with their world view. Practitioners of alchemy and other kinds of occult sciences have come to believe that orgone may be the mystical substance that governs the miraculous. Who knows?

Above: Dr. Wilhelm Reich, originator of the theory of orgone energy. According to Reich, orgone energy, which comes from the sun and is present in all organic matter, accumulates in the genitals during orgasm. Afterward, it flows into the rest of the body, ensuring a healthy body in addition to a healthy mind.

Above: Reich, wearing a checked shirt, explains to a group of students how his orgone motor works. Once Reich had conceived his theory of the importance of orgone energy, he concentrated on finding ways of gathering it for use in the treatment of disease. Eventually he was prosecuted for ignoring an injunction to prevent him advertising and selling orgone boxes or accumulators—the invention that he hoped would revolutionize treatment by focusing orgone power.

Right: Reich's orgone box or accumulator. The box consisted of an outer wooden layer that attracted orgone, and an inner metal layer that reflected the orgone onto the person sitting in it. Over a period of time, large amounts of orgone built up, with supposedly beneficial effect.

The Reason for Cults

Does the history of cults, in all their astonishing diversity, tell us anything about the nature of human beings? At first glance, the cult picture appears so complex that no conclusions can be drawn from it, other than the trite observation that "It takes all kinds to make a world."

The thoughtful observer can, however, discern several themes running through the phenomenon of cultism that point up some fundamental human needs. In varying degrees most cults offer their followers four prizes: a sense of identity, discipline, knowledge, and power.

The knowledge people seek in cults is almost invariably something they cannot find in their society's schools. It consists of "truths" that are presented as either more profound and mysterious than the allegedly superficial and utilitarian learning available in the schools, or simply true where the schools' teachings are false. In the vociferous claims of the flat-earthers, hollow-earthers, and orgone enthusiasts we can hear not only the delight of having discovered the Truth but also a combined sense of triumph and defiance toward the opposing, generally accepted beliefs. In the guarded revelations of the Freemasons and other secret societies we find a deep conviction that they possess a treasure that makes life meaningful as it can never be for the uninitiated. To belong to a cult is to know something that others cannot or do not wish to know, and this gives the cultist a sense of superiority.

It is only a short step from knowledge to power. Implicit—sometimes explicit—in the teachings of many cults is the idea that the follower can use his knowledge to attain power. It may be power over his own body or power to direct his thoughts, as in some of the Eastern cults. It may be power to heal or to see visions. In some cults, such as the Agapemonites or Father Divine's Peace Missions, followers have been promised the power to live forever. The promise of magical powers has lured many people into witchcraft covens in recent years. Within highly structured cults there is plenty of opportunity to wield power over other members. A person who is a very small cog in his company, or perhaps bullied by his wife, may be able to compensate within his cult by attaining a position of authority over others. In the small minority of cults dedicated to violence we find the lust for power in its extreme form. One suspects that the violence itself may even be less exhilarating to such cultists than the knowledge of the fear they inspire in outsiders. The fear with which society once regarded the Thugs and the Assassins, the fear lately generated by Manson's butchers, must be as intoxicating as a drug to those who do the terrorizing.

Although the desire for power may be the prime attraction for some cultists, it is likely that the sense of identity gained through a cult has an even wider appeal. Particularly in the relatively fluid society of Western countries, in which people often move from one locality to another and from one social class to another, a sense of who one is and where one belongs is often lacking. A cult can provide a person with a ready-made identity. If it is an ancient society with a large membership it can give him a sense of importance he might otherwise lack; if, on the other hand, it is a relatively small organization, regarded by outsiders as a "crank group," it will tend to attract people who enjoy the feeling of being part of a despised elite. The outsiders can be dismissed as too stupid or too stubborn to see the light, and their contempt may intensify the feeling of solidarity within the cult.

The sense of identity offered by a cult is almost always tied in with some kind of discipline or submission. Duties imposed on members will have as one of their purposes the strengthening of the members' awareness of being part of a whole. In countries such as the United States, where great importance is placed on getting along well with others, this aspect of cultism can become very prominent. Some cults place greater emphasis on devotion to the leader, particularly if he or she is the founder. We have seen this phenomenon over and over in the messiah-centered cults, and to a lesser extent in those, such as the early Theosophical Society, that have a dominant personality at the top. Many people, it would seem, have a strong need to submerge their own personalities in something or someone stronger than they are.

Fundamentally, what a cult offers a person is a direction for his life. The search for knowledge, power, and identity can be made by oneself, through study, meditation, work, and human relationships; but it can be a difficult and sometimes lonely search. Through membership of a cult, one can make the journey over well-trodden paths with plenty of company.

Picture Credits